More Praise for *Beyond Words*

"We often seem to forget that we began our earth journey without spoken words, yet we are perfectly able to speak the language of the wind, of plants, of animals. Marta Williams shows us that we still can. The link that was severed so many years ago between us and the others survives in a timeless, wordless kind of communication that Marta explains simply, convincingly, and comfortingly. Her sources are excellent, her grasp of the topic of animal communication rich and deep. *Beyond Words* is a balm and a validation for those of us who have always known that there were languages deeper and more enduring than the ones we learned in school."

— Susan Chernak McElroy, author of
Animals as Teachers and Healers and *All My Relations*

"In this deliciously heartwarming book, Marta Williams shares endearing stories of not only her own successes in communicating nonverbally with animals but also the triumphs of her clients and students. This book should be required reading for everyone who lives with a four-legged or feathered friend. *Beyond Words* will bless your life with insights so magical they read like a fairy tale. But here is God's secret, whispered quietly in our ears: these stories are *true*, and animals everywhere are trying to speak to us! It is up to *us* to learn to listen. Marta shows the way! Read this beautiful book and treasure it!"

— Amelia Kinkade, author of *Straight from the Horse's Mouth*

"Through telling the stories of her students' and clients' experiences, Marta Williams gives her readers the experience of learning the power of the connection and healing that take place between humans, their animals, and all of nature. But she goes beyond that, offering her readers the opportunity to have their own personal experiences by doing the exercises throughout her book. Bravo, Marta! You have inspired us all."

— Carol Gurney, international animal communicator and author of
The Language of Animals

"I applaud Marta's pioneering research and her discoveries of how the bond between animals and humans opens a door between our worlds, connecting through the universal language of telepathic communication."

— Carolyn Resnick, natural horse trainer
and author of *Naked Liberty*

"Marta's compelling vision of our world takes a giant leap forward with this book. Through examples of people who have successfully learned and applied the principles she teaches, Marta makes intuitive communication with animals accessible to us all. This wonderful book offers an important opportunity to better understand the animals who mean so much in our lives."

— Allen and Linda Anderson, authors of *Angel Dogs*, *Angel Cats*, and
Rainbows & Bridges: An Animal Companion Memorial Kit

Praise for *Learning Their Language*

"Animals have senses that transcend our five, and it is within this realm that true communication with all life occurs. This wonderful book by Marta serves as verification of and instruction in the magical world of animal communication."

— Marty Goldstein, DVM, holistic veterinarian and author of
The Nature of Animal Healing

"In our society's blinding addiction to reason, our intuition has nearly been extinguished. Allow the message in this book to rekindle your inner connection with all life."

— Julia Butterfly Hill, activist and author of
The Legacy of Luna and *One Makes the Difference*

BEYOND WORDS

BEYOND WORDS

Talking with Animals and Nature

MARTA WILLIAMS

Foreword by Marty Becker, DVM

New World Library
Novato, California

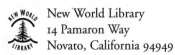

New World Library
14 Pamaron Way
Novato, California 94949

Text design and typography by Tona Pearce Myers

Library of Congress Cataloging-in-Publication Data
Williams, Marta.
Beyond words : talking with animals and nature / Marta Williams.
    p. cm.
Includes bibliographical references (p. 189) and index.
ISBN-13: 978-1-57731-492-9 (pbk. : alk. paper)
ISBN-10: 1-57731-492-1 (pbk. : alk. paper)
   1. Pets—Behavior. 2. Human-animal communication. 3. Animal communication. 4. Conduct of life. I. Title.
SF412.5.W55 2005
636.088'7'019—dc22   2005012959

♻ Printed in Canada on 100% postconsumer waste recycled paper

New World Library is dedicated to preserving the earth and its resources. We are now printing 50% of our new titles on 100% chlorine-free postconsumer waste recycled paper. As members of the Green Press Initiative (www.greenpressinitiative.org), our goal is to use 100% recycled paper for all of our titles by 2007.

First printing, September 2005
ISBN-10: 1-57731-492-1
ISBN-13: 978-1-57731-492-9
Distributed to the trade by Publishers Group West

10 9 8 7 6 5 4 3 2 1

This book is dedicated to animals and to nature.
For far too many millennia they have been besieged
by a human race that has forgotten its origins
and forsaken its nonhuman relatives.
May this book help to change that.

CONTENTS

ACKNOWLEDGMENTS

I promised I'd let them retire in peace, but once again I enlisted the aid of my parents, Jean and John Williams, for their excellent editing abilities. I'm still buying them dinners with no end in sight!

Everyone at New World Library is a joy to work with. My editor, Georgia Hughes, has been a huge support, and her suggestions greatly improved the book. Alexander Slagg and Kristen Cashman were very helpful in the final editing process. The design staff, Mary Ann Casler and Bill Mifsud, turned out another beautiful cover, and Tona Pearce Myers did a great interior design. Monique Muhlenkamp makes publicity fun, which is no easy task, and Munro Magruder has been a sage guide through the foreign land of book marketing.

I had a lot of help in my research on indigenous cultures and intuition, and I wish to thank: Ed Castillo, Sonoma State University; Walter Greist, former psi researcher; Members of the Society for the Anthropology of Consciousness, including: Tina Fields, Matthew Bronson, Marliene Dobkin De Rios, Michael Wink, and Hoyt Edge; Dr. Robert Morris, University of Edinburgh; Connie Grauds, President of the Association of Natural Medicine Pharmacists; Lowell Bean, author; Reno Franklin; and Catherine Held. If Moonhawk were still alive I'd personally thank him for his incredible mind and the wisdom he gave us.

My cat Hazel claimed my in-box as her new bed and curled up right by my side during the many months of writing. When in doubt I turned to her for help, as she is the best feline coauthor a human could ask for.

Hazel

The people, animals, and landscapes you will meet in these stories are the substance of this book. I thank each of them for being willing to share their lives with you. Their experiences confirm that a magical and far better world is possible.

FOREWORD

*I*f you have picked up this book, you are in for the rare double-treat of education and adventure as you explore the magical connections among nature, animals, and humans. In these pages, Marta Williams recounts some of her own stories and the experiences of her clients, students, and friends that demonstrate the profound and effective ways that animals communicate with us when we not only look but *see*, not only listen but *hear*. With this awareness and openness, it's like you're putting on 3-D glasses to view the same thing you've seen a thousand times, only now it's vivid, connected, and spiritual.

Throughout my years as a veterinarian working with animals and their human caretakers, I have witnessed many similar occurrences of strong and vital interactions. Animals fortify us daily with their gifts of unconditional love, limitless affection, and to-die-for loyalty. Our four-legged and winged brethren, as well as the creatures that inhabit our oceans, have much to offer us, and this book skillfully demonstrates how we can tap into their wisdom and love.

Marta presents these stories in a down-to-earth manner and gives suggestions for experimenting with intuitive communication. She addresses questions of accuracy and skepticism directly and thoroughly and provides excellent sources and documentation to support what many of us have perceived yet not always acknowledged: that we truly can communicate as equals with animals and the other beings of the natural world. *Beyond Words* was written for people like me who love animals, nature, and true-life accounts. The stories cover the gamut of working with animals, from training animals using intuition, to listening intuitively so we can understand how to help them heal or assist them during death, to how animals can help us heal physically and emotionally. In my own life experience and work, this link has been demonstrated again and again as animals find just the right people who need them at just the right time, and vice versa.

So now I invite you to read the stories yourself and reflect on your own experiences with the generous animals that share our world. Read about Melissa and her border collie, Aspen, and how Melissa learned to understand and remedy Aspen's mistrust of her husband, and how dolphins off the coast of Hawaii performed a healing on a photographer. Share the joy of a town that came together to rescue a dog separated from his family during a cross-country trip, and celebrate the bond between Neil and Feste, a Morgan–quarter horse cross, who helped a young man mature and taught valuable lessons of comfort and companionship. By telling these stories, Marta invites us to our connection with animals and nature and use this ability to help heal our world. With awareness and openness, we can tap into the wisdom and love that waits patiently for us to embrace and accept it.

— Marty Becker, DVM, co-editor of
Chicken Soup for the Pet Lover's Soul

BEYOND WORDS

THE FIRST LANGUAGE

*T*here exists within each of us an ability to communicate intuitively with animals and nature — to actually converse with other life forms by mentally exchanging thoughts, emotions, and images. I believe this is an ancient, innate characteristic of all life. It is the first language, the foundation of spoken and written words, and the common link between all species. We are born with this ability, but in our modern world we are subtly conditioned to repress it as we grow up. There is little room in the logical modern mind-set for the sometimes vague and often emotional messages conveyed to us by our intuition. Yet even after years of conditioned suppression, we can recover our intuitive skill, which is what I did and what you can do. It's both interesting and significant that at this critical time on earth, when we have gotten so out of balance with nature and estranged from other life forms, millions of people are now drawn to the idea of connecting intuitively with animals and nature.

Intuitive communication is not the same as reading body language, such as knowing that your cat wants to go outside because she's hanging out at the door staring at you. This is something completely different, something that conventional science holds to be impossible — the ability to send and receive thoughts, images, feelings, and other sensory data mentally, without using any sound or gesture, even over a great distance. Here's an example of how it can work: Using intuition, I help people find lost animals. I got a call about a lost animal from Diana Beim, who lives in Half Moon Bay, a town about 150 miles south of my home in Northern California. She'd recently moved to another house, and her cat, Mocha, had escaped from the new place. I asked her for the new address and for a description of Mocha, then hung up and tuned in to Mocha. To do this I closed my eyes and relaxed, forming a mental picture of Mocha and imagining her as if she were right there in front of me.

Once I felt a visual and emotional connection, I introduced myself to Mocha and explained that Diana had sent me to find out how she was and where she'd gone. I then began receiving messages from Mocha. First she sent me words mentally. In my mind I heard her say that she was alive, okay, and not too far away. I asked her to show me, using mental pictures, where she was and how she got there. Almost immediately I saw images of her route as if I were watching a movie. They were transmitted as if through Mocha's eyes. She showed me images of herself going out through Diana's backyard, down a slope, across a creek, and up onto a road. She turned to the right and continued down the road past about five houses, until she came to a gray house. She showed me an image of a shed or garage with brickwork and a flat corrugated roof. She said she was hanging out near the gray house but not going inside, and that she was being fed. Then she sent an image of an older couple. I got the feeling from her that the people who were feeding her were nice and that they had cats of their own. She also showed me an image of a field with a water tower and many colorful plants.

When I relayed this information to Diana she said the terrain descriptions were accurate, and she recognized the road. She said the field would have to be one of the commercial flower fields at the end of the road, an area she had visited on horseback.

Diana rode her horse out to search in that area but could not find the brickwork shed with the corrugated roof that I had described. She did see the water tower in the flower fields and called for Mocha, but she got no response. She ended her search that day by dropping off flyers at all the houses along the end of the road.

The next day she got a call from a woman who lived at the end of the road in a gray house and who had seen the flyer and had been feeding Mocha in her backyard. When Diana went to the woman's house, she discovered a shed next to the house with brickwork and a corrugated roof, which had not been visible from the road. That was where the woman and her husband had been feeding Mocha, who had eluded all their attempts to touch her. Diana confirmed that the couple had several cats, which was what Mocha had told me. When Diana called for Mocha, she appeared from the bushes, ran right to her, and jumped into her arms.

I know this sounds like magic, but I am certain that this ability is real. Someone living in an indigenous culture untouched by the modern world would likely have found this story quite sensible and logical. In such an individual, the extrasensory ability to communicate mentally and from a distance with other people or with animals was probably commonplace. Though we in modern civilization have almost no awareness or acceptance of such abilities, I believe them to be innate and to represent the true nature of human beings.

If you'd asked me fifteen years ago whether I thought humans could talk intuitively with animals and other forms of life, I would have said, "Wouldn't that be great!" I'd always been fascinated by science fiction novels like *Dreamsnake*, by Vonda McIntyre, in which the main character could converse freely with a snake using mental telepathy.[1] But I'd never thought it was anything more than fantasy. When I learned that there was someone in my area who actually taught classes in animal communication, I rushed to enroll in the course. I took every class offered and read every book I could find on the subject, the best of them being J. Allen Boone's classic work, *Kinship with All Life*.[2]

At that time in my life, I had been working for over a decade as a scientist in environmental regulation and toxic-substance control. I earned a bachelor's degree in resource conservation and a master's degree in biology and had worked for several governmental agencies and environmental consulting firms. With such credentials and experience my future was promising, but something just wasn't right. The work I was involved in was important and beneficial, yet I had a nagging feeling that it was not what I should be doing.

Discovering intuitive communication turned everything upside down; I realized life did not really work the way I had been taught. Here was a new and amazing phenomenon that I felt compelled to explore. I had a persistent notion that intuitive communication was something vital that the world was missing, a key to unlock a process that would be exponentially more beneficial to animals and the earth than anything I was doing at that time.

Eventually I decided to change my career and become a full-time animal communicator, someone who uses intuitive communication to assist people and animals. Friends and relatives thought my decision was crazy, and in fact I did take a big risk financially, but I could not deny the pull I felt. I didn't abandon my scientific career, however. To my mind, this field is at the forefront of scientific inquiry.

After years of practice and research in this field, I was eventually led to write a book, *Learning Their Language: Intuitive Communication with Animals and Nature*, which is a step-by-step how-to guide. My intention in writing it was to make the subject accessible and acceptable to a broad range of people, with the hope that readers would be able to use the book to start communicating with animals all on their own. I have gotten many calls and emails from people who were able to do just that. One in particular, from Cathy Isbell, was rather amazing.

Cathy was one of the participants who emailed me during an online chat I did about animal communication. The next day she contacted me again. She said she'd been reading my book and wanted to tell me about an experience she'd had. As I read her email I realized that she was one of those people whom I call "naturals" at intuitive communication. Using only the instructions from my book, she was able to do experiments that clearly confirmed the existence of intuitive communication and her ability to do it.

The animal in the story she related to me was a friend's rottweiler, named Amanda. Cathy encountered the dog tied up outside the local gym one day and stopped to talk to her. She told Amanda that she was a beautiful dog who had a very nice mom. Cathy said she then focused on the dog to see if she would get a response. And in fact, she did. She mentally received the following message from Amanda: "I know I am really the most beautiful rottweiler, but I am worried about my mommy. My mommy is so tired, she fell asleep on *my* bed." Cathy said that as she heard Amanda's words she also got a mental picture of her friend lying asleep across a dark plaid dog bed.

Cathy doubted the image, because she just couldn't picture her friend falling asleep on a dog bed. Just at that moment her friend came out of the gym and walked over to Amanda and Cathy. Cathy asked how she was doing, and her friend responded that she'd been so busy lately, she was totally exhausted. Cathy asked her if, by any chance, she had been falling asleep in strange places. Her friend looked at Cathy curiously and replied yes, that she had in fact even fallen asleep on one of Amanda's dog beds. Cathy could not believe what she was hearing; what she'd heard from Amanda had been correct! Cathy then asked, "You mean Amanda has more than one dog bed?" "Yes," her friend replied. "Amanda has three colored dog beds." She told Cathy that the one she fell asleep on was the plaid one in the living room.

Amanda's people now refer to Cathy as Amanda's aunt, because Amanda is always thrilled to see Cathy and runs across the parking lot at the gym to greet her. They say that Cathy speaks Amanda's language.

That Cathy was able to do this merely with some basic instructions from a book is testimony to the fact that these abilities lie just below the surface of our awareness, completely developed and accessible to us. Being able to hear animals speak in this way is not something only a few gifted people can do; it is a gift we all possess but are unaware of.

The main technique that Cathy employed to be able to hear Amanda is deceptively simple. After she spoke to Amanda, she relaxed and focused inside, paying attention to every single impression that came into her awareness, whether it was a feeling, a memory, an image, or words that popped into her head. She acknowledged and trusted the information, even when it seemed unlikely or illogical. And most important, she was courageous enough to check the information's accuracy.

I always tell people in my workshops that they may need to have a few dramatic experiences, like the one Cathy had, before their skeptical minds will allow them to believe in intuitive communication, or to recognize that they themselves are capable of it. Practicing is key to reactivating your intuition, and it is important to practice in a way that you can receive verification and validation, as Cathy did. Having by now taught thousands of people to do this, I can assure you that everyone is capable of learning.

The book you now have in your hands has a different role from my earlier one. It is meant to help bring humans back into balance with the rest of the beings on this planet. Rather than an instructional manual, this book is a collection of stories, which I hope will convince you that animals and the other beings of the natural world are sentient and have thoughts and feelings just like we do. Many of the stories are testimony to a spiritual evolution rarely credited to animals and contradictory to the normal concept of animals as inferior to humans. The tellers of these stories speak about animals and the denizens of the natural world as teachers, healers, and guides.

When I was about halfway through writing this book, I realized that I had actually envisioned it more than ten years ago and had promptly forgotten about it. I was at a friend's house and said to her, "Wouldn't it be great to have a book with pictures of people with their animals and stories of what happened when they communicated intuitively?" We both agreed that it would be nice and then dismissed the idea, because we had no clue how to implement it. This, then, is the embodiment of a dream that did not intend to be relinquished, expanded to include people's relationships with wild animals and nature as well.

The people who told me their stories talked about dramatic changes that occurred in their lives once they experienced intuitive communication. When confronted with such undeniable evidence of something so unusual, people can undergo a radical shift in consciousness. Indeed, that is the quality that most attracted me to this work. A radical shift in consciousness is precisely what the world needs right now.

I knew I would have to present a story for the introduction of *Beyond Words* that would immediately convince people that there was something to my claims. Soon after I had that thought, the following incident occurred.

I was teaching an intermediate workshop in animal communication and had taken the students to my stable to meet my horse, Dylan, and the other horses there. (See photo on back cover.) The students each chose a horse to practice with. When they finished we all met in Dylan's stall to discuss the results. Dylan's stall is quite large, so we were able to stand in a semicircle around him. One student, Jennifer Freudenberg, told us that the horse she'd talked to had given her the name and description of his person. Jennifer recounted what the horse had said and asked me if the information was correct. I was happy to be able to tell her that it was, but as I spoke, my horse did something odd that I had not seen him do before, nor have I seen him do it since.

Jennifer was standing with her shoulder next to Dylan's, and as I spoke, Dylan moved a few steps closer to her and put his cheek right against Jennifer's. The rest of us were spellbound. Dylan kept his cheek there for about three minutes. Then he stretched his head out in front of Jennifer and began yawning. He yawned three or four times and then hung his head, looking sleepy. Everyone asked me what Dylan was doing, and I was at a loss for an answer, because the behavior we had witnessed was completely out of character. Dylan is friendly, and he will calmly tolerate humans fussing over him, but he's not a super-affectionate horse. He's not one to move in close and rest his cheek on you. I had to bribe him with treats to teach him to give me kisses, and he still does it readily only if I clearly have a treat or am thinking of giving him one.

"Well," I said, "I've heard horses will yawn to release emotions, so it must have something to do with that." No one had anything else to add, so we finished up at the stable and went back to my house to continue the workshop. I gave the students another exercise to do, and while they were working I took the time to tune in intuitively to Dylan and ask him what the heck he had been doing with Jennifer. He told me that Jennifer was frightened, and that when I confirmed her information, she got very scared. Dylan said he helped take away her fear.

I waited until the next exercise was finished and told Jennifer what Dylan had said. I asked her if that was actually what had happened from her point of view. She said yes. She said she had known from an early age that she had lots of intuitive ability, but it was very frightening for her. When I verified her answers at the stable, she said her whole body froze with fear. Then she confirmed the information I'd gotten intuitively from Dylan — after he touched her cheek and yawned, her fear had gone away.

All the stories I present in *Beyond Words* have this element of the fantastic or unbelievable. Yet they are true-life encounters told to me by students, clients, colleagues, friends, and family. You will be able to see some of the storytellers in photographs and learn about them through the details they gave me in interviews. You may notice that most of the storytellers are women. This does not reflect a personal bias or a lack of effort on my part to include stories from a more diverse group. I think it is just a mirror of culture. Most professional animal communicators at present are women. My assessment of this is that women are expected, and therefore allowed, to be more emotional and more intuitive than men. Women are also considered to be less logical than men, so it is less surprising that they would profess to be able to talk intuitively to animals. The social taboos against men are more stringent. One of my students asked me not to tell anyone that he has studied with me or to call him at work. He is quite good at communicating, but he doesn't want anyone in his life to know about it. I don't believe these differences between men and women are inherent, but I do think such characteristics have been culturally induced. Men can learn to communicate intuitively just as well as women, though they might have to work a little harder to get around their own internal blocks to the process.

The women in this field are predominantly white, which is, I believe, a function of the class structure of society. However, as the field becomes better known and more accessible, a greater diversity of practitioners are being attracted to it.

This attraction stems from our memory of the intuitive connection to animals and nature we had when we were young, which each of us wants to recover. Ecopsychologists would probably agree with this analysis. Their new field of psychology looks at the self in relation to nature. According to ecopsychology's main proponent, Theodore Rozak, we all are conscious on some level of the onslaught against nature and our precarious position on the earth; we just have chosen denial as a defense mechanism for dealing with this knowledge.[3] Conversely, on some level we all want the earth to be healthy and life to be secure again. Learning intuitive communication to reconnect with nature facilitates a harmony we are all unconsciously longing for.

I did a lot of research for this book, because I was curious to find out what others had to say about the prehistoric roots of intuitive communication and its prevalence in contemporary indigenous cultures. From the time I started in this field, in 1989, I've felt that intuitive communication was a natural ability common to all people, integral to indigenous cultures, and key to creating balance between humans and nonhumans. In my research I looked for corroboration. I found some fascinating little-known authors, most of whom are now deceased, who gave this subject a great deal of thought. Some even conducted field research on the subject. I share their findings in chapter 1, "The World Beyond Words." In that chapter I also explain how intuitive communication works, and give some basic techniques for you to try. To learn this skill in depth, I recommend you read my first book, *Learning Their Language*, which provides detailed instruction and verifiable exercises.

In arranging the stories of this book, my intent has been to lead you on a journey similar to my own. Initially, I questioned the authenticity of intuitive communication and had to have several remarkable experiences before I became convinced. In chapter 2, "Crossing the Line," I include one of my own stories and stories from other people that provide undeniable evidence for the validity of intuitive communication.

One of the first experiments I tried with intuitive communication was to use it to find my lost cat Marmalade, and I was successful. Chapter 3, "Connecting through Crisis," relates stories of people connecting intuitively with animals in the midst of a crisis, often with profound results. Chapter 4, "Lessons in Living," encompasses the wise teachings that come about from connecting intuitively with other life forms.

My life was irrevocably changed by following this path. I have met some of the best people on the planet, I suspect, and have journeyed much further physically and spiritually than I ever expected to. In chapter 5, "Transformations," I include stories of others whose lives were similarly transformed.

Chapter 6, "Practical Magic," is a study of the amazing results that can come from the practical application of intuitive communication, from finding lost animals to training a horse.

In my previous book I touched on the subject of reincarnation. For this book I decided to treat the issue more directly. I have collected a batch of stories that I find to contain convincing evidence that animals are able to reincarnate and do come back into our lives. See what you think when you read them yourself in chapter 7, "When They Return." In chapter 8, "Spiritual Journeys," I tell the stories of several of my students who, like me, decided to devote their lives to the study and practice of intuitive communication, and the journeys that led up to their decisions.

I titled the last chapter "A Better World Is Possible" because

I believe it is. I am not being naïve. As an environmental activist I am well aware of the problems we face. In my view, the systems of government and commerce worldwide are maladaptive and need to change. Because I work with animals, I am aware of the overwhelming pain and suffering they endure. I realize how big the problems are, and I have devoted myself to finding ways to address them. Often when people begin studying intuitive communication, their hearts open up to the overwhelming suffering of animals and the earth, and they go into true emotional and spiritual crisis. Chapter 9 addresses that condition and is intended to help show the way through the darkness. I view reconnecting with animals and the earth as an essential step in the journey to a better world. I also know that real action in the real world is crucial, and I will give you my best advice for how to do that successfully without burning out.

Another factor in this business of getting from here to there, of moving from a world of alienation and disrepair to one that is sustainable, fair, and healthy, involves spirituality and the emotional and energetic techniques you can use to bring your dreams for yourself and for the world into reality. I will tell you everything I have been able to learn so far about this. Interest in intuitive communication continues to grow worldwide. I believe this is because the animals and the earth want us to connect with them again, the way our ancestors did. I'm sure we will have to do this if we wish to restore our balance with nature and survive on this planet. I hope that *Beyond Words* will help you reconnect with this ancient skill.

In his book *God Is Red: A Native View of Religion*, Vine Deloria Jr. writes of an intimate connection between Native Americans and nature that was lost when Europeans invaded North America and decimated the indigenous populations as

<table>
<tr><td>CHAPTER
ONE</td><td># THE WORLD
BEYOND WORDS</td></tr>
</table>

*O*ne day, Natasha Downing called to ask me to talk intuitively with her dog Louie, a ten-year-old standard poodle–golden retriever cross who looks like a white English sheepdog. I had spoken with Louie a few times before, when Natasha wanted me to ask him his opinion of the latest groomer she had taken him to, among other things. Groomers are a subject of enormous concern to Louie. He has a difficult time with them, but he has to go because his coat is so luxuriant. Normally, I do consultations right on the phone or have clients make an appointment to call me back. But on that day, I had a lot going on. I promised Natasha I would talk to Louie as soon as I had a chance and would call her back to report.

As it turned out, I did not find time to talk with Louie until about five thirty that evening. He and I talked — from a distance, intuitively — for about twenty minutes. Louie told me he liked his latest groomer. I called Natasha around six o'clock to give her my report. She immediately wanted to know what time I had spoken with Louie. She explained that Louie had stopped eating in the middle of his dinner, around five thirty. He had gone over to sit by the sliding glass door and was still staring off into space, refusing her efforts to coax him back to his food bowl. Such behavior was completely out of character. Louie had never before stopped eating in the midst of his dinner. I didn't get the impression during my talk with him that Louie was upset about anything. Natasha and I concluded that it must have related somehow to my intuitive conversation; we laughed about it and hung up.

Half an hour later Natasha called me back. Louie still wasn't eating. Not only that, her other dog, Lela, a ten-year-old golden retriever, had stopped eating too, and was sitting beside Louie, staring out the door. Natasha could see nothing going on outside, no noise or movement in the backyard. At this point she was getting worried.

I decided this was a great chance to conduct an experiment. I asked her to hang up the phone and tell Louie that I said I was finished talking with him, and he could eat the rest of his dinner now. I asked her to call me back after she had done that. She called right back to say that as soon as she relayed the message, Louie and Lela went straight for their dinner bowls and resumed eating. I could only conclude that Louie was just waiting to see if I intended to say anything else, and Lela was helping out.

Fortunately, this was an unusual episode, but one that does suggest the validity of intuitive communication. There simply was no other explanation for Louie's atypical behavior. In more than fifteen years in this field, I have had thousands of experiences that corroborated the authenticity of intuitive communication. It would be impossible for me now to deny the existence of a complex and sophisticated world of communication between humans and other species that transcends the spoken word. But I started out as a skeptic, so I understand others' disbelief. It took me a long time to finally be convinced. I needed to have proof because of my scientific background, and I set about getting it by conducting experiments, asking questions of animals that I could then verify through the animals' people. Eventually I amassed enough evidence to win over my internal critic. The stories in this book may provide you with sufficient confirming details, or you may have to conduct some experiments of your own. Here is another story to consider.

In my beginners' workshops on animal communication, I teach my students that they can send a message to an animal, even from a distance, and the animal will receive it. That's because animals are masters of intuitive communication. Like us, they are born with the ability to communicate intuitively, but no one ever teaches them that it's not possible, so they remain excellent receivers all their lives. We, however, have to relearn how to receive intuitive communications. A student from one of my beginners' workshops, Nancy Duquette, decided to conduct an experiment while she was at work. She mentally contacted her cat, Junior, and sent him the thought and image of him curled up on her stomach with his head on her chest. Junior had always done that in the past, but for some reason he had recently stopped, and Nancy wanted him to start doing it again. When she got home from work her husband said, "Junior did something really weird today. He got in my lap and then crawled up and put his head on my chest. Can you believe it?" Junior had never before done that with anyone but Nancy. When they compared notes, Nancy discovered that Junior went to her husband's lap shortly after the time she had mentally sent the thought and image of that behavior to the cat.

HOW IT WORKS

Intuitive communication is based on an inherent ability common to all people. It encompasses the skills associated with extrasensory perception (ESP) and psychic ability. Most people can relate to the idea of intuition and have had hunches or gut feelings about things, such as whether to trust a stranger they've just met, whether to take a job offer, or whether someone is angry with them. Intuition is a useful survival tool, but most people have almost lost touch with it. Logic and reason are favored by modern culture, and we are actively discouraged from using or developing our intuition. We retain it in our adult life, but we are usually not aware of it. When it surfaces, it's often during a crisis — to inform us of some threat or critical event, such as an ill or dying relative. Intuition also speaks to us in our dreams.

Animals recognize the survival value of intuition, and they never disconnect from their intuitive sense. They are constantly scanning the environment for intuitive data, alert for any changes, such as shifts in the emotional states of those around them. In her book *And the Animals Will Teach You*, psychologist Margot Lasher credits her dog with saving her life on two occasions, when he intuitively sensed and alerted her to danger.[1] If your otherwise trusting dog starts acting suspicious of a stranger, take heed: your dog is probably sensing something you aren't. Animals are experts at this ability; we can best learn to hone the skill ourselves by employing them as our teachers.

Intuitive communication is not a logical process. It can be done at great distances, and you do not have to actually see or know the animal you wish to speak with. Information is exchanged in a nanosecond, and unlike with human speech, many people can talk intuitively to the same animal at the same time without any worry about noise or interference. Information is sent via one of five modes: hearing, feeling, seeing, smelling, and tasting. These modes parallel our five senses but are like phantoms of those senses. Following is a description of each of these modes, with examples of how they function in the process of receiving information intuitively.

• **Feeling.** Receiving feelings means being able to perceive the emotional or physical state of another, for example, sensing someone's mood or being able to discern whether a person is feeling ill. This ability is also known in the field of parapsychology as *clairsentience*, or clear feeling. It parallels our sense of touch, but functions more as an extension of it.

Karen Berke, a student of mine, told me a story about picking up information empathetically. Right after a cold rain, she walked by the stall and paddock of an elderly horse at her stable and felt an overwhelming sense of depression. She said it was as if the horse were saying, "I can't go through another winter." Karen knew the horse was being well cared for and thought the message was just her projection based on her feelings about the weather until two days later, when she found out that the horse had died and realized the horse had been sending her that information.

• **Hearing.** Hearing words mentally is known as *mental telepathy*, the mental exchange of words and thoughts, or *clairaudience,* clear hearing. To send a message to an animal mentally, all you need to do is think the content of the message, focus on the animal, and intend that your message be received.

Here is an example of a very effective sending event. A client of mine, Geoffrey Levens, decided to try an experiment with an animal after reading my first book. His cat, Willie, often rubs against people's legs to convey a desire for food and has all the humans trained to put more food in his bowl at this signal. One day, as Willie was doing his rubbing act, Geoffrey said, "Hey, if you want food, why don't you go point at your dish instead of coming to me?" Willie instantly stopped, gave Geoffrey a long strange look, and turned and walked toward the dish. As he approached the dish he froze midstride, like a pointer spotting a bird. Willie got a lot of food that day.

But Geoffrey discovered that this technique has its limitations. He has been trying for years to get Willie to stop bringing gophers in through the cat door and ripping them up on the carpet. His main response initially was to throw Willie back outside with the gopher. But Willie would come right back in, forcing Geoffrey to lock him outside. He tried pleading with Willie to keep the gophers outside. He issued stern threats. Nothing worked. Then he tried taking the gopher away and not giving it back, at the same time praising Willie for being a great hunter. Geoffrey told Willie if he kept the gophers outside, he could keep them forever. But these talks with Willie backfired: Willie now thinks that Geoffrey wants the gophers. When he gets a gopher, he races into the house, seeks Geoffrey out wherever he is, and drops the gophers at Geoffrey's feet. Fortunately for Willie, Geoffrey really loves him.

The opposite of this procedure is *receiving* words and thoughts mentally from an animal. This can be much harder to do, because the words and phrases coming in will be difficult to separate from your own thoughts and internal dialogue. It can sound like you talking to yourself. To overcome this barrier, practice with many animals, using questions that can be verified by each animal's person. This is the quickest and best way to check out whether you are receiving accurately.

• **Seeing.** Exchanging visual images mentally is called *clairvoyance*, or clear seeing. These images will appear in your mind's eye. You don't actually see the images; you get a mental picture.

When I work with finding lost animals, I frequently see images of where they are or where they have been. In one case of a dog lost in another state, I tuned in intuitively to the dog and saw in my mind's eye an image of an elevated bridge and a muddy, boggy area where I believed the dog had traveled. It turned out there was such a bridge with a marsh nearby, and the lost dog was later sighted in that area.

The intuitive sense of clear seeing also occurs when you get a clear sense of certainty about something. An example of this occurred when my holistic veterinarian, Lisa Pesch, lost her cat, Bella. Bella had run off just a few days before Lisa was to move to a new house. Lisa has studied animal communication, so both of us tuned in to Bella to find out whether she was alive and where she was. Each of use got the distinct impression that Bella was okay, but upset about the move, and that she was somewhere near the last house at the end of Lisa's street. I sensed that Bella was up high and wondered if she might be on a hill behind that house. When Lisa went looking, she found Bella high in a redwood tree in the backyard of the last house on the street. It took a tree climber to get her down.

• **Smelling.** Perceiving a smell mentally is a virtual experience. You don't actually smell anything; you are just suddenly aware of, say, the odor of cigarette smoke (an odor a lot of animals send to me and complain about). The ability to perceive a smell intuitively is also called *clairallience*, or clear smelling, and it is not usually as strong as the other modes.

I recall one student who received intuitive information primarily as smells, from which she would then form various conclusions about the animal. For example, she would receive the fragrance of green grass and go on to say that the horse she was talking to wanted to eat grass but couldn't because he never left his stall. The information she got turned out to be accurate, even though her mode of reception was quite unusual. Her case is one reason why I now tell students that it really doesn't matter which mode you use. You can communicate well in any of the five modes.

• **Tasting.** Perceiving a taste mentally is called *clairhambience*, or clear tasting. As in the case of virtual smelling, you don't actually taste anything; you just become aware of a specific flavor. I guess I have to include a disclaimer here: Be careful what you ask for intuitively! In one of my teaching exercises, I suggest that students ask their animal to send information intuitively in every mode; that is, to ask the animal to send a feeling, a word, an image, a smell, and a taste. One woman's cat sent her the taste of a gopher, which the woman all too successfully received.

Signatures of Intuitive Information

There are three characteristic signatures of intuitive information:

1. The information comes in quickly, sometimes even before you can complete the question.

2. The information you receive is so odd that you think it must be wrong, and you know you could not have made it up yourself.

3. You have an absolute, unshakable feeling of certainty about the information.

If any one of these conditions is present, you can be fairly certain that you are dealing with information that has been intuitively derived.

COMMUNICATING WITH NATURE

I have alluded to but not actually addressed the concept of talking with something other than an animal. Am I suggesting that you can talk to a tree? Yes, and further that you can converse with every aspect of nature — trees, plants, waterfalls, lakes, the wind, and the land. In Native American cosmology, the earth and everything on it is considered sentient. Standing Buffalo (Tatanga Mani), a Stoney Indian of Alberta, Canada, expressed this attitude in a speech he gave in London in the late 1960s:

> Did you know that trees talk? Well they do. They talk to each other, and they'll talk to you if you listen. Trouble is, white people don't listen. They never learned to listen to Indians so I don't suppose they'll listen to other voices in nature. But I have learned a lot from trees: sometimes about the weather, sometimes about animals, sometimes about the Great Spirit.[2]

Herbalist Karyn Sanders recounts that her Choctaw grandmother taught her to ask permission of a plant before harvesting it for use as medicine.[3] The plants did not always agree to be taken, and their wishes were to be respected. Lucy Smith, a Mihilakawna Pomo elder, expresses the idea that every part of nature is alive and important when she discusses her mother's teachings. Her mother told her:

> We had relatives...and we all had to live together, so we'd better learn how to get along with each other. She said it wasn't so hard to do. It was just like taking care of your younger brother or sister. You got to know them, [found] out what they liked and what made them cry, so you'd know what to do. If you took good care of them you didn't have to work so hard. Sounds like it's not true, but it is. When that baby gets to be a man or woman they're going to help you out.
>
> You know, I thought she was talking about us Indians and how we are supposed to get along. I found out later by my older sister that mother wasn't just talking about Indians, but plants, animals, birds — everything on this earth. They are our relatives and we better know how to act around them or they'll get after us.[4]

Two botanists, George Washington Carver and Luther Burbank, claimed to talk with their plants and receive responses in exchange.[5] Carver, most famous for his innovations with the peanut, the sweet potato, and the soybean, credited the plants with all of his inventions and claimed they had described to him how they could be used. Burbank talked with his plants and sent them feelings of love every day. He was convinced that they understood him. Perhaps one aspect of the genius of each of these men was a willingness to step outside conventional belief and practice.

In her book *Jungle Medicine*, Connie Grauds tells of how plants transformed her life.[6] At the beginning of her story she describes herself as a pharmacist with a conservative midwestern upbringing who works at a major HMO — a most unlikely person to end up talking to plants. But through a series of curiously related events, she traveled deep into the Amazon, met a shamanic healer, and eventually spent some years as his apprentice. Midway through the apprenticeship she began to hear plants speaking to her mentally, telling her what they could cure and what she should use them for. When it first happened she thought she was crazy, but as she tested out each communication from the plants and discovered the information to be accurate, she finally came to believe that plants can think and communicate.

Several researchers in the United States and the former Soviet Union came to the same conclusion after working experimentally in the laboratory. Cleve Baxter is famous for his experiments wiring plants to a polygraph and then monitoring readings when the plants were subjected to various direct and indirect stimuli.[7] Pronounced reactions from the plants were observed when a leaf or stalk was cut off. The plants reacted even when people standing near them would simply think about cutting a stalk. Soviet researcher Venyamin Pushkin wired plants to an electroencephalograph (EEG), normally used to study brain waves, which measures the electrical responses in the skin. In his experiments, a person sitting near the plants was hypnotized and then given suggestions ranging from the positive (imagine a sunny day at the beach) to the negative (imagine being out in a snowstorm). The plants were observed to respond in sync with the human subject. As a control, Pushkin conducted many sessions recording the plants' reactions in the absence of human contact, or when the human was in a neutral emotional state, and he saw no observable responses. He concluded:

> Thus it appears that the psyche of man, however complicated — our perception, thoughts, memory — all this is only a specialized development of an information system that already exists on a rudimentary level in plant cells.[8]

The problem with communicating intuitively with plants, trees, a lake, or a mountain, is that any data you get back will be hard to prove; it's much easier to verify information received from animals. I found that once I had enough validation of my own communication with animals, it was easier to accept the notion of communicating with other elements of nature. Now I relate to everything in nature as a sentient being, with whom I can have a conversation of equals. I suspect this is close to an indigenous mind-set, and possibly the way life is really supposed to be.

INDIGENOUS CULTURES AND INTUITIVE COMMUNICATION

In her work on Old Europe, the Bulgarian archaeologist Marija Gimbutas described the prehistoric culture of that region as egalitarian, peaceful, and nature worshipping. Her analysis of prehistoric culture is based of necessity on interpretation of archaeological evidence.[9] Other authors have put forward similar descriptions of the worldviews of prehistoric cultures in North and South America.[10] Vine Deloria Jr. recounts that one Cayuse leader, Young Chief, refused to sign the Treaty of Walla Walla because he felt the rest of creation was not represented in the transaction.[11] Indisputably, prehistoric cultures were much more connected to the natural world than modern cultures are.

In the research I conducted, I was curious to find information specifically on indigenous cultures' use of intuitive communication. Such information is not easy to come by for a variety of reasons. First, most existing indigenous cultures have been severely altered by European conquest; it is difficult to find one that has remained unmodified by exposure to modern culture. Calvin Martin conducted a masterful study of the decline of indigenous culture in his book *Keepers of the Game*.[12] Working with historical texts, he re-creates the destruction of the traditional culture of the tribes along the eastern seaboard of Canada following conquest by Europeans. These vibrant native peoples went from being healthy and in balance with wildlife and the environment to disease ridden and utterly dependent on the European fur traders for survival. The balance and mutual respect they had had with wildlife was eroded, and the situation degenerated into the wholesale slaughter of millions of animals, practically exterminating the beaver and, in the West, the buffalo.

A second difficulty in uncovering information about intuition in primitive cultures is that such cultures were poorly studied by anthropologists, who saw claims of telepathy or other intuitive powers as childish magical thinking and dismissed them without ever considering their possible validity. I did manage to find a few researchers who addressed the issue. In his work on California Indian shamans, for example, Lowell Bean states:

It is generally assumed that whatever has life has intelli-
gence. Thus the shaman may communicate with...all
living things, and even seemingly inanimate things...a
rock for example...animals, birds, trees, grass, flowers,
wind or water. The shaman may know the language
of these. And with them...he or she communicates
regularly.[13]

In the 1950s, Ronald Rose and his wife spent seven years
among aboriginal tribes in Australia, studying and documenting
their claims of intuitive abilities.[14] The cultures they studied were
already falling apart, and today fully tribal groups may no longer
exist. At the time, however, Rose found a ubiquitous ability
among all those he studied, for sending and receiving information
intuitively over long distances. In cultures like those of the Australian aboriginal tribes, which were separated by vast distances,
it makes sense that people would have a highly developed ability
to communicate in this way. Most often, Rose found, the information an individual received had to do with an illness or the
death of a family member; much of the data was corroborated by
witnesses outside the tribe, such as missionaries or cattle ranch-
ers. It is interesting that sometimes the individual would receive
the information by conversing with a totem animal rather than
from direct mental contact with another person. The people Rose
studied also claimed to possess the ability to make rain, control
storms, cure illness, travel out of body, shape-shift, and cause the
death of another (which was done to someone who had committed rape or violated another strong taboo). The research Rose
conducted will probably never be replicated or matched, since as
he himself pointed out, there are so few tribes left to study.

Adrian Boshier, like Rose, specifically set out to evaluate the paranormal, in this case in a primitive African tribe. His research, conducted in the 1960s, was funded by the Parapsychology Foundation of New York.[15] Boshier was able to verify that the African witch doctor with whom he ended up apprenticing was an adept intuitive, able to connect with animals intuitively and predict their behavior. She also was able to accurately foresee events in Boshier's future and images of events that had occurred in his past.

The research of Rose and Boshier was well documented and credible. Both researchers cited extensive personal observations and numerous collected anecdotes. Their work firmly supports the idea that intuition was an integral aspect of indigenous culture.

HOW IS INTUITIVE COMMUNICATION POSSIBLE?

Most scientific disciplines do not concede that intuitive communication is possible, with the exception of the field of physics. In physics, the idea that we can be aware of and affected by events taking place at a distance from us is referred to as *quantum interconnectedness* or, alternatively, as *nonlocal correlation*. This theory was put forth by several researchers, including Albert Einstein, in 1935. The classic physics experiment cited as evidence of nonlocal correlation is the observed behavior of two photons originating from the same source and traveling in opposite directions. Scientists observed that each photon is affected by what happens to the other, even after they have been separated by a great distance. In his book *Limitless Mind*, physicist Russell Targ likens this behavior of photons to the behavior observed in identical twins who, though separated at birth, share almost identical tastes, interests, experiences, personalities, and professions.[16] Targ is one of the preeminent researchers in the field of intuitive, psychic, or as he terms it, "psi" ability. He worked for many years with the U.S. military, training people to use intuitive ability to find downed planes and kidnapped dignitaries. The military's term for this activity is *remote viewing*. Many of the military "viewers" became so adept that they were able to remotely locate Russia's hidden missile silos. The locations they pinpointed were verified after the cold war ended.[17]

Targ states in *Limitless Mind* that the statistically based research proving the existence of remote viewing has a one-in-ten-billion chance of being false.[18] Unfortunately, Targ's research has received little attention from mainstream scientists. Other interesting facts that Targ reports are that intuitive ability (or remote viewing) is not bound by space or time.[19] In other words, you can intuitively tune in to any place or any being on the planet at any time in history. Targ argues that the more accurate way to view our universe is as a hologram, a concept put forth by David Bohm in his book *The Undivided Universe*.[20] In a holographic model of the universe, each region of time and space contains information about every other region of time and space. There are no boundaries, and all information is instantly accessible everywhere and always.

Targ's book is fascinating, and one of the best on this subject. He concludes that the key to experiencing these phenomena is *intention*. Having the intention to do remote viewing or intuitive communication is all you need in order to get started. To perfect your skill, you just have to practice.

USES OF INTUITIVE COMMUNICATION

Intuitive communication is becoming popular worldwide because it can be very helpful. You can use it to negotiate with feuding animals, help a timid animal to trust, enhance an animal's training, find out about an animal's past owners and experiences, or find a lost animal. You can use it to discover an animal's feelings, wants, and needs, which is especially useful when the animal is old or in poor health. By explaining to your animal a situation such as an upcoming move before it occurs, you will help allay the animal's fear.

Intuitive communication can also be used to communicate with wildlife. Some people have had great success in politely asking the gophers to move or the ants to leave. I've talked with many gardeners who profess to use this skill to discern their plants' needs and desires, thereby keeping their plants healthy and happy and creating a more harmonious garden. You will see for yourself in the stories in this book how practicing this skill has had important effects on many peoples' lives. It may do the same for you, should you decide to pursue it. On a larger scale, were more humans to begin relating as equals to other species, there would be a profound and far-reaching benefit to all life on earth.

ACCURACY AND VERIFICATION

Intuitive communication can be very accurate. However, to prove this you have to be able to check your data. One way to do that is to set up verifiable experiments, asking questions of animals you do not know well and then checking your answers with the animals' people. In beginning workshops, I ask participants to connect intuitively with an animal they are not familiar with and ask the animal what his or her home looks like. People get astoundingly accurate details about houses they have never seen.

You will read many stories in this book about people who received information intuitively from an animal that they were later able to verify. With all the animal communicators now practicing in the world, the body of verified instances of intuitive communication is probably vast. Yet no matter how accurate or detailed the anecdotes, modern science seems unwilling to accept the validity of this field. Skeptics claim that the communicator is reading an animal's body language and making other assumptions based on prior knowledge of the breed or species. But when a person is able to take a photograph of a dog sitting in an open field, connect with that dog intuitively from a distance, and discern that the dog lives in a two-story brick house with oriental rugs, a sunken living room, a yellow kitchen, and mostly white furniture, then the animal's body language, breed, and species are irrelevant. I rarely work with animals in person or even see a photograph of them, so reading their body language would not be an option.

Other critics suggest that communicators are asking leading questions of their clients and feeding back the information the client has supplied. I am sure there are people who do this, if even unconsciously, and it is something communicators need to guard against. One way I do that is by doing some of my consultations directly with the animal without the human client's presence or participation. In those cases I have clients give me the name, age, sex, breed, color, and physical description of the animal, and have them tell me what the problem is or what they want me to explore. Then I hang up the phone and contact the animal. There is no possibility of quizzing the client to uncover the information that I receive.

The anecdotes I have collected convince me that the process of intuitive communication is authentic. It is not, however, infallible. There are times when your own bias can influence your results, such as in the case of a lost animal who could be living or dead, when you would much prefer that the animal is still alive. Interference from personal bias, or any form of physical or emotional stress, can cause inaccuracies. Even the best human intuitives do not claim to be more than 80 to 90 percent accurate, on average. When you are working with your own animals, it can be more difficult to check accuracy. Usually, the proof will be in their actions. Do they act as if they heard you? Did what they told you turn out to be true?

A client of mine, Tery Pierson, related two instances when her horses' behavior confirmed that they had heard her. The first happened one day after her horseshoer had finished working on one of her horses' feet. He turned the horse loose in a pasture with other horses, whose feet had not yet been shod. When Tery discovered this she said to her horse, "No, I don't want you with those horses. They haven't had their feet done yet. I want every horse whose feet have been done to go over to that pasture over there." Without any further prompting, and to the astonishment of the horseshoer, Tery's horse trotted into the other pasture.

She got confirmation again a few days later with both of her horses, a mare and a gelding. Normally she fed the mare her grain in the stall, and the gelding would run in and start eating the mare's food. On this day Tery said to him, "Wait on your side and I will bring your food right out." She was thrilled when he stayed in the paddock and waited for her to bring him his food.

I especially like stories in which an animal stops eating and does something atypical in response to an intuitive communication, because animals who love to eat usually don't inexplicably change their eating behavior unless they are ill. They are too fixated on their food to have any presence of mind whatsoever!

A fellow animal communicator, Lena Swanson, told me about a problem she was having with her golden retriever Naca that she resolved just by talking to the dog. Naca had started running away during walks and getting pushy with other dogs. Lena told Naca the changes she wanted to see and explained that noncompliance would mean having to go to a dog training class. She said Naca's behavior improved overnight.

THE OTHER SIDE OF SCIENCE

Apart from the physicists, there are a few researchers from other disciplines who are open to the possibility of intuitive communication. Among these is Rupert Sheldrake, a British microbiologist, who has focused his complete attention on this field. Using statistically supportable research techniques, Sheldrake proved, with very little probability of error, that animals can predict when their owners are coming home. His book *Dogs That Know When Their Owners Are Coming Home* is about this and other intuitive or psychic phenomena in animals.[21] Sheldrake also identifies the dilemma that despite a lot of public interest in the subject of psychic and intuitive ability, little corporate or governmental funding is devoted to research into the topic.

Most scientists cannot accept the existence of intuitive communication any more than they can accept the premise that animals are as intelligent in their own manner and method as are humans. Or that animals have emotions so close to the quality and intensity of our own as to be indistinguishable. Or that animals have souls and are capable of noble actions. Instead, science views everything an animal does as the result of rote behaviors dictated by genetics and instinct. The only emotions allowed to an animal are said to be driven by the animal's desire to perpetuate its own genetic material. The drive to survive genetically is supposedly what motivates animals to compete, nurture, socialize, and assist others. The idea that all this is ludicrous does not need to be explained to any genuine animal lover. Animal lovers know that animals can read our minds even if we can't read theirs. And most animal lovers fervently believe that animals are not only highly intelligent, but also more altruistic and unconditionally loving than are most humans.

A HOLISTIC APPROACH

At first, I did not realize that in my research on this subject what I was actually seeking was a holistic approach. When I was directed to the work of Dan Moonhawk Alford I discovered an eloquent and brilliant theoretician who had given a great deal of thought to intuitive communication (which he terms, alternately, *psi* and *telepathy*), relating it to aspects of indigenous culture, quantum physics, linguistics, and parapsychology. He calls this integrated field of study *quantum linguistics*. Moonhawk (his Native American name) corroborated my thesis that intuitive communication is the prototype for language. He identifies it as the "old language," used by preconquest indigenous cultures and the vehicle for communication between all life on earth. Unfortunately, I discovered his work two years after his untimely death from cancer. Moonhawk was earning a PhD in linguistics at University of California at Berkeley and had studied physics. He had spent time with the Northern Cheyenne and Navajo, learning both languages and eventually teaching Navajo on the reservation. As far as I know, his work is not in print. I found it through my research on the Internet, and I believe it is available only online.[22]

Moonhawk felt that no concept of language would be complete unless it included the idea of old language. He saw intuitive communication as a basic flow of meaning and perception, a primitive form of knowing. He defined being able to read the emotional intentions of another as a system of information transfer that predates the development of speech and provides the foundation of language. He claimed that without the continuing unconscious operation of the old language in the background of our consciousness, our speech would make no sense.[23] The limitations of current models of linguistics, he stressed, are that they do not allow for telepathy as an active factor in human communication.[24]

Moonhawk was a student of indigenous languages and identified them as key to indigenous thought and worldviews. In his analysis of the Cheyenne and Blackfoot Indian languages he noted that they are more kinesthetic than the verbal-visual European languages. A speaker in Blackfoot could talk all day about riding horses without using a noun. Rather than an image of riding a horse, the speaker would be conveying the body feeling and emotional experience of riding a horse. Moonhawk felt that these indigenous languages closely approach intuitive communication. The difference between the two, he explained, was that in European languages the dancer is valued over the dancing; in Native American languages, the dancing is valued over the dancer. He concluded that in indigenous culture and language,

> processes and interrelationships are more real than the "things" that grow out of them — that the physical is an epiphenomenon of the non-physical, and that cyclical timing is more real than linear time. We need both descriptions for a complete picture of how reality works for everyone, as well as [descriptions of] how language works for everyone on this planet. The Middle Way, as the Chinese termed it, is a difficult road to even FIND, and especially in our newfangled, ultra-gadgety world. Yet finding it and balancing ourselves will become even more important as we face what is to come in the next decade or so as we approach what the Mayans called the beginning of the Age of Consciousness.[25]

Suggested Practices

SENDING

Try this experiment: Talk to your animal out loud as if he or she understands you completely. If you already do this, skip ahead to the receiving experiment.

When you do this experiment, try to suspend your disbelief and adopt an innocent curiosity instead. You are doing this to see what will happen. Over a period of two weeks, talk to your animal out loud as much as you can. Tell him or her how you feel about things, or how your day went, just as you would converse with a person. Politely ask your animal to change any behaviors that might be bothering you, and if there is something you would like your animal to do, ask for it, just as you would ask a person. You can also try bargaining with your animal — "I'll do this for you if you do this for me." But be sure to keep your end of the bargain!

Keep a written record of any changes you note in your animal's behavior. If your animal complies with your requests and suggestions, be sure to give lots of feedback and appreciation, also out loud, just as you would to a person.

Many people who try this exercise discover that it works so well they make it a permanent change in the way they relate to their animals. At a minimum, I recommend talking out loud to your animals to explain any changed circumstances or potentially stressful activities before those events occur. That gives the animals a "heads up" and an opportunity to adjust to the coming changes. Animals like to be forewarned, just like people do.

RECEIVING

Oddly enough, it can be easier to receive information intuitively from an animal you don't know than from one who is familiar to you. You know so much about your own animals that you may think any information you receive is something you yourself made up. To counteract this tendency, try the following exercise: Ask your animal, "Do you have a question for me?" If a question pops into your head, answer it as best you can, either by talking out loud or sending thoughts. Keep answering questions until the animal is finished. *Don't question the question; just assume it is coming from your animal.* If you are successful, you will bypass your inner critic and experience what it feels like to receive information intuitively. You may also find that you and your animal end up in a back and forth discussion of a subject that your animal has chosen, which is the goal of the exercise. If your animal does not have a question or you just don't get anything, let it go and tell your animal you will ask again another day.

CHAPTER TWO	CROSSING THE LINE

*H*earing amazing stories about intuitive communication may not be enough to convince you of its authenticity. Actually *having* an undeniable communication with an animal yourself probably would. Stories were what convinced me that intuitive communication was possible, but it took a personal event to show me that I could truly do it myself. I call it my "Jenny experience."

One day, when I was just starting out in this field, I came home from work and the skeptical friend I was living with asked me to talk to my cat Jenny and find out what she had done that day. So I went to Jenny and asked her. A picture flashed into my mind of Jenny up on the ledge of my backyard fence, touching noses with a squirrel. I was surprised at the image, as I had never seen Jenny do anything like that, but I decided to go ahead and describe it to my friend. He stared at me in shock, then said that was exactly what Jenny had done that afternoon. This single incident turned the corner for me. I would not and could not have made up that image. From that point on, I knew I had the ability to receive messages intuitively from animals, and I never looked back.

The stories in this chapter are about people who also had experiences that were undeniably convincing. When an animal tells you something that you had no way of knowing beforehand, and it proves to be accurate, you cross a line into another reality. Your awareness shifts, and you realize that it is possible for every living thing to have consciousness. After my Jenny experience, I found I became more careful to avoid hurting other living things, and I began using speech and reasoning as methods of problem solving with my animals. I also discovered that wild animals, trees, and the landscape could convey messages and wisdom. I think what happens when one learns this skill is that one experiences a shift in consciousness, back to the mind-set of ancient people and the way they perceived nature.

RELUCTANT RACEHORSE

I met Reverend Marian Hale at a lecture I gave in Chicago one winter. After the lecture, I got a ride with Marian to where I was staying. She told me a little about her work as a minister, including performing weddings and other ceremonies. She said she had studied psychic ability and was hoping to attend the workshop I was teaching the next day if she could get away. She asked whether it would be all right if she arrived late, and I said it would be no problem.

Marian arrived right after lunch, just as the class was beginning an exercise. The students were dividing into pairs and exchanging photographs of their animals. Marian paired up with Joel Kahling, who gave her a photograph of his horse, Blue, a bay Thoroughbred gelding who had once been a racehorse. I outlined a series of questions to ask the animals, then led the students through stages of relaxation and focusing. I asked them to connect with the animal in the photograph by imagining the animal right in front of them. Then I told them to introduce themselves to the animal and make sure it felt okay to proceed. At that point I said, "Raise your hand if it doesn't feel okay, and I will come help you." I rarely have anyone raise a hand at this point, and everyone in the class seemed fine, so I said, "All right, go ahead and ask the questions." Just at that moment Marian raised her hand.

To keep from distracting the class, she and I went over to a far corner of the room to talk in whispers about what was wrong. Marian told me that when she contacted Blue, she received a clear but frightening image of him. He had bared his teeth at her and then turned and tried to kick her. She said she could tell he was angry — furious, actually — and she didn't know what to do. She seemed genuinely shaken. I advised her to go back in, tell Blue that all she wanted to do was help him, and ask him to tell her what was wrong. She sat with her eyes closed for a few moments and then opened them and said in a whisper, "Marta, he is showing me a number that he has on his gum. He is curling his lip up and showing me a number on his gum. He said they made him a slave when he was a racehorse and he hated it. They put a number on him. What should I say?" I did not know why the horse was behaving that way and wasn't sure what to tell her. I just said, "Tell him that you will tell Joel about this, and ask if Blue would be willing to answer your other questions now." She conveyed the message to Blue, and he agreed to answer her other questions, so I suggested she go back to her seat and finish the exercise.

Once the students were ready, I had them check their answers with their partners, and then we had a discussion of their results. Most people discovered that the information they'd received from the animals was accurate.

When Marian began telling Joel about Blue's behavior and the number in his mouth, Joel interrupted, saying, "Oh, not again!" Joel told us he had had three separate animal communicators talk to Blue in the past, and Blue had conveyed the same message to each of them. Joel explained to the class that racehorses are tattooed on the lip with a number, something neither Marian nor I had been aware of until that day. Blue did in fact have a tattoo in his mouth, though on his lip, rather than on the gum, where Marian had seen it. And Blue had, in fact, told three other communicators that he hated the number and felt he had been enslaved. Marian and I were stunned at how precise her data had been. She knew nothing about horses, let alone racehorses, and she could not deny that this information had come straight from the horse's mouth!

She and I discussed this off and on for a few weeks following the class. She said that the entire experience had shattered her basic, society-driven beliefs about what is possible and what is not. She believed in animal communication, but to have a direct experience with such clarity and vividness was disconcerting. She decided to speak about it to others, because she did not want to bury it and go back to her previous beliefs; she wanted her experience to be the basis of a new view of the world.

Marian was concerned about Blue's state of unrest and asked me what could be done. I explained to her that one of the things that happens when you open up to feeling the world, which is really what intuitive communication is about, is that you open yourself to the pain of other species. There is no way around it. To go into intuitive communication means to be willing to live with the dissonance, and commit to doing what you can to improve life for individual animals and promote respect for the earth. It is good to learn how to exist and function in empathy with all life. But it isn't easy! I told her she could stay in contact with Blue intuitively and reassure him that his racing days were over.

Joel contacted me several months later to report that Blue was doing much better; he was acting a lot happier and seemed finally to have gotten over his tattoo issues.

Marian shared one other story with me about her cat, Homer, who is pictured in the photo on the next page. Homer was a very small and graceful Abyssinian cat. He slept with Marian every night, snuggled up to her belly as she lay on her side, curled around him. Even when Marian shared her bed with a lover, Homer would creep under the covers as soon as their breathing deepened into sleep, and he would still be there in the morning. Through marriage, divorce, and several tumultuous relationships, Homer was Marian's constant companion — uncomplaining, unruffled by anything, and always present for her. Marian said he would often gaze at her with his huge, round, unblinking eyes. She said that when he did this, she felt in her heart that he was saying, "You are wonderful, Marian, and you are my friend. I accept and love you completely."

For many of those years with Homer, Marian was a heavy drinker, finding herself depressed by both her home and her work situations. She finally stopped drinking in 1985, and a few years later she decided to have a complete physical examination to find out how much damage had been done. When she met with the doctor to get the results, he asked her how many years she had been drinking. She told him twenty years. The doctor said that was hard to believe, because her kidney and liver functions were fine. Her results were unusually good for a heavy drinker, he said, and he had quite honestly been expecting to have to give her some bad news. She celebrated the results with a decaf coffee and a hot fudge sundae.

Around this same point in time, Homer started to go into a decline. Abyssinians often live into their twenties, but he had begun to weaken when still much younger than that. When she took him to the veterinarian for testing and treatment, she was surprised at the results. The veterinarian told her that

Marian and Homer

Homer did not have long to live. Marian could not believe it; he looked so sleek and healthy. The veterinarian agreed that Homer looked fine on the outside but said that his liver and kidneys were failing rapidly.

Homer lived only a few more weeks after that. Marian is sure that on some level Homer had been helping to process all the toxins she had been ingesting for so long. Then his body finally gave out. Marian said that she understood all too well how animals can be our teachers and healers. Homer was her best friend, and she misses him still.

BLACKY

Irene Bras lives in Rotterdam, in the Netherlands. I met her when I taught a beginners' workshop there. Fairly quickly I realized I had quite a skeptic on my hands. To almost everything I said, Irene would respond, "Yes, but how do you know this is true? I find it hard to believe." Irene was studying to be an anthropologist, which I'd have thought would make her a bit less tense. Don't anthropologists have to be somewhat open to and accepting of other cultures and unfamiliar ways? But Irene questioned and critiqued everything. I had to work hard to get her to acknowledge that she was successful with the exercises, and that she was actually getting accurate data from her communications. She conceded that I had a point, but it took a couple of years for Irene to fully convince herself of her ability. The following story describes her turning point.

Irene volunteers at a cat sanctuary. One day one of the cats, a black male named Blacky, started to limp on one of his front legs. It turned out that he had a malignant tumor. The veterinarian

Irene and a cat from the sanctuary

proposed either giving Blacky painkillers for a while and then euthanizing him when the pain got too bad, or immediately amputating the leg. He was not in favor of amputation, because he suspected the disease had already spread, and he feared Blacky wouldn't be able to survive in the sanctuary: Cats there aren't caged, and the forty who live there walk freely around the cat house; the veterinarian thought that with only three legs, Blacky wouldn't be able to defend himself.

Irene decided to contact Blacky directly, using intuition, to ask him how he was feeling and what he wanted. When she did so, he was very clear that he wasn't ready to go. He told her he still had a lot of work to do at the sanctuary. He also wanted "that which does not belong to me" to be removed quickly. Irene didn't know if he would understand that his whole leg had to be removed, but when she explained it to him she got the feeling he understood perfectly well and was glad to make such an offering in order to be able to live on. When she asked him if the disease had already spread, he said he was almost sure it had not. He added that they would have to act quickly, and then he showed Irene an image of his lungs filled with red spots. Irene understood the image to indicate that the disease would start spreading to his lungs soon. Blacky also told her that he would manage perfectly well among the other cats with only one front leg.

After the conversation Irene contacted the veterinarian to tell him to go ahead and amputate Blacky's leg. The veterinarian agreed reluctantly, warning again that the disease had probably already spread to Blacky's lungs. His remark was actually positive feedback for Irene, because she had not known this was a possibility until she'd heard it from Blacky himself!

The leg was amputated a few days later. Blacky recovered from the operation extremely well and easily adapted to walking on three legs. The other cats didn't start to bully him; instead, he radiated authority. Even the biggest fighting cat in the bunch respected him! As of this writing, more than two years after the surgery, Blacky is still managing perfectly, and the disease has not spread. Irene is convinced that without intuitive communication, this wonderful cat would have been euthanized.

This experience, Irene said, was the deciding one for her. After Blacky, she became a complete believer. She sent me the following note:

Thank you for helping me make the first steps on the road to a better world in which people will realize they aren't the masters of nature but a part and on an equal level with the animals and plants. This class made me see that even I can get in contact with the "illogical" side of my brain. You tempered my critic and succeeded in cracking this "tough nut."

Crossing the line to the realization that intuitive communication is authentic and verifiable has had a profound impact on Irene's life. She said it changed her relationship with her animals, deepening the bond between them. She also began to feel a need to share her knowledge and experience with others. She began to offer consultations, teach workshops, give lectures, and stage public performances. She gave up her career goal of becoming an anthropologist. Instead, she and her partner decided to work toward establishing a center to promote animals and nature. In Irene's words, learning this skill "transformed my entire life and gave me the opportunity to find out who I really am and what I would like to achieve in this lifetime."

Irene has become a prolific and skilled communicator. During a workshop I held on communicating with nature, she had an unusual and interesting experience. The premise of the workshop is that one can connect with all life forms using intuitive communication: not only animals but also trees, other plants, and aspects of the landscape. Irene chose to talk with the water in the slough that encircled the children's farm where we were studying. She said it was a very special encounter. She sat down next to the water and, without planning it, she placed her hands above it, palms facing down, which is traditionally a healing position. She wasn't really expecting communication; she thought she might just get a feeling of peace. But the water did start to talk with her. She said it sounded like many voices and spirits speaking as one. The voices of the water told her all was not well, because of worldwide pollution. The spirits of the water were thrilled to receive healing from Irene, and she said she could feel something like tiny hands envelop her body and caress her. The voices told her they were very sad and didn't know how much longer they could hold on. They stressed that they were of vital importance to everyone, because they brought and sustained life. They said it was of the greatest importance that human beings become more aware of this and start paying them more respect. They asked Irene to visit them more often, because they liked her company and the healing she offered. Irene said this conversation made her realize yet again that no matter how big a problem might be, one shouldn't feel desperate or helpless. Everyone can make a difference.

MR. MOUSE

Nancy Stephens, a client from Ontario, told me her own crossing-the-line story, about a mouse. One day she was moving a pile of wood, and when she lifted the last board, she found a nest of mice. The mice scattered everywhere, except for one. A tiny mouse with huge round ears and big eyes stayed and looked up at her. She said, "Don't worry little one. I won't hurt you." The mouse seemed to respond to her words and she felt that the mouse wanted to interact with her. The impression she was getting was that the mouse wanted to be touched, so she reached down and patted it. The mouse let her rub behind his ear for a few moments. He even turned his head up, like a cat does, so she could get at the best spots. When Nancy stopped scratching, the mouse started to walk away. Then he stopped and looked back at her, and she felt he was saying he wanted more, so she reached down to scratch behind his *other* ear for a few moments. When he was finally satisfied, he left. Nancy was amazed that a wild animal could interact with a human this way and that she could so clearly and accurately perceive the mouse's thoughts.

A NANNY FOR TIGER LILY

One day I got a frantic call from Geneva Smith, a horse breeder in Texas, asking for assistance with a quarter horse broodmare named Tiger. The mare had recently foaled, but because of an old hip injury she was having trouble taking care of her baby, Tiger Lily. Because Tiger could not keep up with the herd out on the pasture, Geneva had to put the mare and her baby in a small paddock. Tiger was severely depressed, and her baby was getting no exercise at all. Geneva did not know where else to turn.

I spoke with Tiger, and she told me she wanted another horse to help her take care of Tiger Lily. I asked if there was one horse in particular, and she showed me an image of a light-colored mare that I thought was a buckskin. Tiger said if she could get help with her baby from this other horse, she would be okay. I told Geneva what Tiger had said. Geneva responded that she did not have any buckskins in the herd. The only light-colored mare was a palomino, Holly, whom no one could touch. They couldn't even get her in a halter to give her shots. I told Geneva to just go out to the pasture, ask if any of the mares wanted to help Tiger, and see what happened.

Geneva took a halter and rope, went to the middle of the pasture, and sat down. She announced that she needed one of the horses to come to her and volunteer to help Tiger with her baby. To her astonishment, Holly walked right up to her, lowered her head, and willingly accepted the halter. Geneva could not believe what she was seeing. She thanked Holly and led her over to a larger paddock adjacent to Tiger's. As Tiger and Holly visited over the fence, Geneva got her first sense that everything was going to work out.

Geneva with Holly, Tiger Lily, and Tiger

The mares were doing fine over the fence, so Geneva put Tiger and the baby in the larger paddock with Holly. It worked like a charm. Holly babysat Tiger Lily, Tiger Lily got the exercise she needed, and Tiger's spirits lifted. Once the baby was weaned, Tiger got some needed chiropractic care and other bodywork to help her deal with her injured hip.

Geneva called to tell me the good news, and she said, "Marta, I am a Republican and probably about 180 degrees away from you on just about everything. But you have made a believer out of me. That is for sure."

THE RAT LADY

This story, told to me by Nicole Smith, the daughter of one of my students, Beth Smith, comes from her experience in the Peace Corps in the Republic of Kiribati, north of the Fiji Islands. The story demonstrates how ancient indigenous connections to nature persist in modern times. Nicole describes the island republic as very isolated; people there still adhere to many of the old, premissionary ways. For example, when the men harvest coconuts, they sing to the trees as they climb, believing that their songs bring energy to the trees and increase production. The church disapproves of this practice, considers it to be magic and therefore bad, and tries to suppress it. But the people continue to do it anyway. Nicole said the islanders are still very much in tune with nature. They rise with the sun, go to bed with the sun, know all the constellations, and correlate the movement of the stars with fruit production.

Large rats live on the island, and to Nicole's dismay, some of them began coming into her house and eating her clothing. While in town one day, she joked about this with some of the Kiribatians. They earnestly replied that she needed to get the "Rat Lady" to come talk to her rats. Willing to try anything, Nicole had the Rat Lady over. The woman moved around the whole house, speaking in a whisper the language Nicole had come to recognize as the pre-Christian language of the island, what the elders called "the language of the spirits." Then the Rat Lady put out a dish of food just for the rats and left. For many months after her visit, Nicole's life was rat free. Then slowly they came creeping back. Whenever that happened, Nicole would call the Rat Lady again, and the rats would vacate the house for another period of months. Nicole said that much of the lives of the islanders revolved around magic. She said she was very grateful for, and a true believer in, the magic of the Rat Lady.

Suggested Practice

Ask your animals to do something or act in such a way as to provide you with indisputable proof that they hear and understand you. You could ask them to do something out of character, such as to stop eating and come give you a kiss. Or you could talk to them about a problem or situation and ask them to behave differently or to help you in some way. Then pay close attention and observe what changes ensue.

CHAPTER THREE

CONNECTING
THROUGH CRISIS

*S*trong emotions facilitate intuition. Some of the most convincing intuitive experiences that people have reported have been coincident with a highly charged emotional event, such as an injury, illness, or the death of a loved one. In such situations, people seem able to sense intuitively what is happening with an animal or person, even in a distant location. Ronald Rose, in his studies of Australian aboriginal tribes, consistently observed this ability to know from a distance when a loved one was gravely ill or dying.[1] Animals also possess this uncanny ability, as Rupert Sheldrake has noted in his book *Dogs That Know When Their Owners Are Coming Home*. Sheldrake presents numerous corroborated anecdotes of animals who began howling or behaving strangely at precisely the moment their human, in a remote location, died.[2] When I ask students in my classes about this type of experience, more than half tell me they can recall at least one such event. Typically, their stories involve a family member who knew intuitively from a distance, without any clues from the environment, when a family pet or a relative had fallen ill or was dying.

I think these experiences are possible because our intuition is always working. It has not atrophied or gone dormant under the influence of modern culture; we have just become very good at blotting it out or ignoring it. When something truly serious, dangerous, or life-shattering happens or is imminent, our intuition sends us strong emotional messages, and we pay attention (or should). It is even possible for our intuition to foretell events of transcending importance, whether positive or negative. The aboriginal people Rose studied often knew days in advance of an impending death or an unscheduled visit from a relative. They received the information when awake or during dreams as persistent feelings, thoughts, and images. Many also claimed to have gotten the news from their totem animal, who appeared either in body or as a spirit and spoke to them directly.

Crisis situations promote a deeper connection among the individuals involved. Many of the stories in this chapter concern extraordinary relationships that developed out of crises. People often seek out animal communicators as a last resort when addressing a crisis they are experiencing with their animal. Through the communication, they discover a whole new way of connecting with and understanding their animal.

COCI

A client of mine, Felicia Wimmer, had a remote intuition experience with her Thoroughbred mare Coci (pronounced KO-Kee).

When she was a teenager, Felicia purchased Coci, who was untrained and would run uncontrollably when Felicia rode her. Felicia started over with ground training and spent quiet time with the mare. She and Coci managed to develop a deep bond and a great relationship, and Coci became Felicia's best friend.

Coci

When she married in 1981, Felicia still had Coci. On her honeymoon, she suddenly became uneasy and upset. She started crying uncontrollably and felt a strong pull to return home. Her husband thought he might be the cause, but she quickly reassured him: her feelings had nothing to do with him; she just felt an overwhelming urge to go home. Neither of them could imagine why she was distressed, so she suppressed her feelings and they stayed on as planned.

When they returned home, her father-in-law was there to greet them. He motioned her husband aside, and in that instant Felicia knew what had happened. Her beloved Coci was gone. She asked everyone, the caregivers and the veterinarian, what had happened. No one had answers. All they could say was that Coci lost control of her hindquarters. Given the horse's age (she was then in her twenties), and since they couldn't reach Felicia, they had chosen to put the mare down. All Felicia had left of Coci was an invoice for the euthanasia.

Death did not end the relationship, however. On a cold winter day some years later, Felicia was talking on the phone with a friend. He told her about an animal communicator in California named Fred Kimball, with whom he'd had some amazing experiences. (Fred, now deceased, was an incredibly accurate communicator and a very humble person. His legend lives on.) She found the stories amusing and, when she hung up, thought that she might try animal communication for fun sometime. Then she walked into the bedroom and stopped short. She could not take her eyes off the portrait of Coci hanging on her wall. It had been there for years, and she'd walked by it many times every day, but in this instant she was riveted. Then she burst out crying. She knew that she would have to call Fred because he would have information and answers for her from Coci.

Frightened, and not knowing what to expect, she called him. She could hardly speak. He put her at ease and told her to give him only Coci's physical description, which she did; she also told him that Coci had died.

Fred then described experiences Felicia and Coci had shared that only she and the horse could have known about. He accurately described what had happened in Coci's final hours. Then he gave Felicia a message from Coci. Coci said she had tried to wait for Felicia but could not hold on. She had tried hard to reach Felicia, but Felicia was too far away. When she received this message, Felicia was overcome with guilt and sadness. Coci's words, "You were too far away," haunted her for years.

Through animal communicators, Felicia had several more intuitive exchanges with Coci, who even butted in during consultations regarding Felicia's current horses. It seemed that Coci still felt the desire to communicate with Felicia and took every opportunity to do so.

These experiences prompted Felicia to try to develop her own abilities to communicate intuitively. Now she talks directly with Coci herself. Coci constantly reminds her that intuitive communication is important and that she should practice more. Felicia said Coci also helped her finally to understand the phrase "You were too far away," which had so distressed her. Coci meant that Felicia had been too far away intuitively and not enough in tune to realize that her horse was dying. This realization has been a powerful reminder to Felicia that intuitive communication is an important aspect of life. Felicia ignored her intuition and lost touch with Coci when it mattered most. She has vowed never again to ignore such intuitive messages.

CHARMING ASPEN

Melissa Lawrence called for a consultation for a crisis she was having with her border collie cross, Aspen. I had helped Melissa and her husband, Rusk, find Aspen about two years before, when the dog had escaped from a pet sitter's home. This time Melissa asked for help with Aspen's behavior. She'd not mentioned it before, but Aspen had always mistrusted Rusk. She would not interact with him or even eat in his presence. The situation had reached crisis proportions, Aspen was now leaving the room as soon as Rusk entered, and Melissa was hoping that I could help.

Aspen

When I talked to Aspen she said she could not bring herself to trust Rusk and would continue to distance herself from him if possible. I concluded that it would be up to Rusk to shift the situation. Rusk was by this time rolling his eyes a bit at the whole concept of my interviewing Aspen about their relationship. However, I could see no option but to instruct him to talk to Aspen out loud, heart-to-heart about the problem, as if he were talking to another human being. I told him to tell Aspen how much he wanted to be her friend and then to visualize the kind of relationship he wanted to have with her. I also told him to send her a feeling of love from his heart whenever he was near her, and to compliment her often. He was to ask Aspen to reconsider being his friend, but tell her he would understand and respect her regardless. I recommended that Melissa also talk to Aspen in detail regarding how she felt about the situation, and suggested they use massage and some other calming aids as well, which I hoped would have a good result.

Melissa called a few weeks later with encouraging news. As skeptical as Rusk had been about talking with Aspen, he nevertheless had made a big effort to do it, and the results were amazing. Rusk was now much less skeptical, and chatted with Aspen almost every day, or gave her a pat and praised her for something or other. Aspen's response to him was positive. She stopped cowering when she was around him, stopped running away from him and seemed to have a sunnier disposition. She also, for the first time, ate food that Rusk offered. Melissa reported that because the crisis between her dog and her husband was resolved, Aspen had become a changed soul.

LADY LUCK

I don't normally help people with racehorses, because I think the racing industry is bad for horses. I made an exception when Nancy Stephens, a client from Canada who is an equine body-worker, called in a panic about a racehorse she was trying to rescue from a life on the track. The mare was Pacific Jewel, a four-year-old trotting horse whom Nancy had been hired to massage. She first met Jewel when the horse was about three years old. Jewel was thin, aggressive, and potentially dangerous. Her eyes were sunken and dull, and she never played. It was obvious that Jewel was frightened, depressed, and angry. Nancy felt that the horse hated being in a stall, which is where she was twenty-four hours a day, and that she hated racing.

Nancy and Jewel

Jewel's new owners could see that the horse was going down-hill, so they sent her to live at Nancy's farm. Nancy gave Jewel bodywork, pasture buddies, twenty-four-hour turnout, and a home atmosphere in which horses were also pets, something Jewel had not experienced before. Jewel began to thrive. She also started winning races.

After about a year, Jewel's new owners decided to sell her. By then Nancy had fallen in love with her. She called me in a panic, because she wanted to buy Jewel but did not have enough money. She was desperate and fearful about what would happen to Jewel under new owners. Jewel knew something bad was happening, and she had deteriorated into worry and withdrawal. The situation could not have been much worse.

I told Nancy every technique I knew of, including visualizations and meditations, for creating an outcome you desire (techniques that I explain in detail in chapter 9). I talked to Jewel and told her how to do these things too. I was Nancy's coach, helping her to regain her calm and balance and work with the techniques and her real-life friends to shift the situation. She had very little time before Jewel went to sale and did not have anything close to the asking price. She did everything I suggested and the situation completely shifted. She found a friend who was willing to be a coowner and advance half of the money, and Jewel's current owners relented and agreed to give Nancy a break on the price. Jewel would now live with Nancy forever.

After she purchased Jewel, Nancy learned that the horse had been raced almost nonstop for three years, ever since she was started as a yearling. Most racehorses work for about six months and then get a break. As soon as she purchased Jewel, Nancy gave her a six-month vacation. Now Jewel's eyes sparkle, she mugs for treats and attention, and she is the leader of the herd. She instigates play and leads races in the field. When Nancy looks into her eyes she feels Jewel saying, "Thank you for seeing who I really am and for letting me be happy." Nancy said Jewel's world now is one of undisguised joy, and Jewel herself has transformed into a sweet, angelic horse. Jewel will still race, but only because she is good at it and only if Nancy feels certain she is enjoying it.

Because of an ultraconservative upbringing, Nancy at first had not allowed herself to fully believe in intuitive communication. The crisis with Jewel gave her both the need and the freedom to pursue it. There were too many synchronicities for Jewel's appearance in her life for it to have been an accident. What's more, Nancy said, the many intuitive conversations she and Jewel had during their ordeal convinced her of, and gave her confidence about, her intuitive abilities. She now uses intuitive communication regularly with all her animals. Every day she and her husband tune in to their animals just as one would talk with family members. Nancy said that Jewel has helped her and her husband discover and explore the spiritual and metaphysical side of life.

CIRCLE OF HEARTS

Star Dewar travels the worlds' oceans to study and photograph marine mammals. She is also a student of animal communication and one of those people to whom animals seem to gravitate, which means she gets some great photographs.[3] She and I have both experienced, and benefited from, incredible connections with dolphins and whales in the wild, and we share the belief that such encounters should not be one-way. It is great to see and interact with these animals, but they need us to reciprocate by actively working to ensure their survival. Star has committed herself to this cause, and she uses her photographs and experiences to educate as many people as she can reach. This is one of many amazing encounters with marine mammals Star has had in her travels.

Star and dolphins

Early one morning, when Star was on a solo photography shoot at Makua Beach, in Hawaii, she heard the pod of spinner dolphins she was planning to photograph pass by. She was still laying in her tent and wanted to get out and go find them, but she could not move. Muscle spasms in her lower back and shooting sciatic nerve pain in her leg had virtually paralyzed her. Star said all her memories of the intense pain of a ruptured disk from years past came flooding back. In tears, she crawled out of her tent and onto the beach. The dolphins had circled back again and were now about a mile from her, flipping, spinning on their tails, and crashing back into the dark, wind-chopped water.

Fighting pain, Star wriggled into her wet suit and fins while still flat on her back in the sand. Grabbing her camera, she pushed herself backward into the surf. Once in the water she could feel the vibrations of the dolphins singing. Raising her head, she could see them on the horizon, performing Olympian leaps. She called to them in her own version of dolphin song while painfully kicking her way past the reef through waves. Crippled or not, she intended to rendezvous with the pod.

Suddenly, out of the blue-black water, hundreds of shadows surrounded her on all sides. The dolphins had raced to see her! Her pain momentarily lost, she became entranced by the dolphins' wild chasing, spinning, and playful gnawing on one another. One dolphin was even scratching another's forehead. Marveling at their willingness to accept her, Star sent out loving energy to the pod and asked them to help heal her pain.

At this point, all the members of the pod disappeared except for one male, who swam right up to Star's face. Then, as suddenly as the others had disappeared, they all returned and surrounded her again, forming a wide circle with several rows below her. Every pod member had become perfectly quiet, almost somber. The dolphins remained in formation, not even rising to the surface for air. Looking down about six feet below her, Star saw nothing but glowing gray backs. The dolphins' haunting songs had dwindled to a whispering whistle. Even the newborns stopped suckling and took their place in the formation of dolphins below her, which was now pulsating with energy.

Star felt her body go limp, and her hips and sacrum seemed to open wide, like the base of a pyramid. A feeling of intense heat rushed down through her body and out the bottoms of her feet. The pain in her leg dissipated and her spine lengthened. She dangled in the water like a jellyfish, relaxed and pain free.

Finally able to kick normally, she swam with the dolphins as they headed out to sea. A male dolphin dropped back to match her pace. Her heart sank when she saw that his whole right side had been torn by what appeared to be a shark attack. She wondered if he had been slashed while protecting his family. Star felt him read her thoughts as he looked right at her and released a long string of little bubbles from his blowhole. Sensing that he too needed healing, Star directed healing energy toward his wound. Once again she felt intense heat surge through her. Her breathing all but stopped. Then she sensed a fleeting caress on her cheek and watched as the dolphin joined the others heading west into the deep South Pacific.

Star looked back to shore and realized she was very far out. Her camp appeared no bigger than a matchbox. She kicked her way toward the beach, thinking that gravity and dry land would be the true test of the healing she'd received. When she reached the sand she stood up tentatively, then was able to straighten her spine without pain. Waving thanks to the dolphins, she stretched her body to the limit. Anyone who has ever suffered from sciatic pain and muscle spasms in the lower back knows that this kind of spontaneous recovery is miraculous.

The scientists on the research team in an adjoining camp dropped their binoculars and clipboards and rushed over to Star as she reached the shore, concerned and curious. They told her they'd seen the pod circling her for two hours, and at times dolphins would jump and flip. They worried that the dolphins might have landed on her, because they lost sight of her snorkel. They also knew that her back was hurting and had seen her crying about it just that morning. What, they wanted to know, had happened out there? Star didn't know how to explain what she'd experienced. She just said that she and the dolphins had had a meeting of hearts.

NEIL AND FESTE

I came into Feste's life in the middle of a crisis that began when he went to the dentist. Pamela Ginger Flood had rescued Feste, a Morgan–quarter horse cross, from neglect and poor treatment when he was in his twenties. Her young son, Neil, who had named Feste (based on the word fest, which means party), was the horse's main rider. Three days before the dentist appointment, Feste stumbled while Neil was riding him. Pamela remembers thinking that the incident did not look like a trip, and she was keeping an eye on him. When she and Neil brought Feste into the barn for his dentist appointment, Feste reared, turned, and fell to the ground before anyone could prevent it.

The attending veterinarian ran over. Feste was having the equine equivalent of a heart attack. People were directing Neil to leave, but Pamela insisted that he stay. She knew how connected Neil was to Feste. Pamela knelt at Feste's pelvis, and Neil went to his head. Pamela spoke out loud to the horse: "Feste, listen to me. We love you very much. If it's time to go, we will understand." Pamela was amazed to hear a voice in her head respond. It was Feste answering her, cutting through the normal barriers to reception because of the urgency of the situation. "No, I can't be ridden," he said. "I am going to hurt my boy. I have to die." Pamela replied, "No, Feste. You will never be ridden again. We want to keep you. You have so much value to us without anyone ever riding you again. You have a home with us no matter what. We want and value you."

At this point Feste's head was down on the ground, and he was very still. Pamela told Neil to talk to him and tell him that he did not care about riding him anymore, that he just wanted Feste to stay around. Feste's heartbeat was dangerously irregular, but she and Neil kept talking to him. After about twenty minutes, Feste lifted his head back up and got to his feet. Neil took that to be a decision and threw his arms around Feste, saying, "Thank you, Feste, for staying. I love you."

The veterinarian had helped keep Feste alive with medications during the uncertain period while he was hovering close to death and Pamela and Neil were speaking to him. Everyone in the barn that day clearly understood that Feste had heard Pamela and Neil, and that he had made the decision to live. The veterinarian told Pamela that Feste had contusions inside his mouth indicating that his liver was not functioning well. She said he might have only a few weeks to live.

From that day forward, Neil spent four hours a day with Feste, brushing, walking, playing, and talking with him. Weeks turned into months, and Feste hung on to life for almost another year.

Pamela called me when summer was approaching because she needed to make a decision about whether Neil should go to camp as scheduled or stay at home with Feste. When I talked to Feste he indicated it would be okay for Neil to leave for a short time. However, once Neil was gone, Feste went into a rapid decline; he stopped eating, drinking, and moving. Perhaps he didn't realize how devastating life would be without Neil, or perhaps he wanted to try to leave without Neil's being present. In any event, he was on his way out. Pamela called me again, in a panic, and asked what to do. Should she get Neil back from camp early to see Feste before he died? Absolutely, I advised. Arrangements were made to pick Neil up, and Pamela gave Feste updates on where Neil was and how soon he would be home. Feste held on. Friends actually observed him begin to walk around again when he was told that Neil was only an hour away.

When he arrived at the ranch, Neil flew out of the car while it was still moving and ran to Feste, flinging his arms around him. Feste was able to walk out of his stall that day, with Neil at his side. He rolled in the round pen and then grazed for hours beside his boy. Only at night was he willing to return to his paddock.

After that, Feste and Neil spent every day together, with Feste grazing and Neil playing. Feste also began wandering around to visit the other horses, apparently saying his good-byes. Pamela bought my book *Learning Their Language* and read the techniques to Neil, who began to have daily intuitive conversations with Feste. Feste asked for Neil's blessing to die, and Neil gave it to him.

Neil and Feste

Eventually, Feste had another more serious attack in which he spun and fell. This time he was injured so badly that he had to be put down. Pamela and Neil were able to explain the process to Feste, and all of them calmly and sadly discussed and accepted that it was his time to go.

Since Feste's death, both Pamela and Neil have studied with me, and both are using their intuitive talents to help animals. Pamela uses her communication skills to help people resolve problem behaviors in their horses. Neil is using intuitive communication to ride horses, in particular a difficult gelding named Midnight, whom most adults would hesitate to mount. Neil said Feste gives him advice about how to ride Midnight, and then Neil talks to Midnight as he rides him.

Neil told his mom that learning to communicate with Feste before and then after the horse's death had completely transformed his life. It had given him an understanding of death as a change rather than an end. Pamela, too, learned something from Feste: she learned that she has a facility for helping horses cross over from life to death. She has since been asked to help dozens of horses go through the dying process, and she in turn calls on Feste to assist her in these cases.

Neil and Feste still have an amazing connection, one that has transcended life itself. Neil feels that Feste is watching out for him and giving him advice. If Neil could wrap his arms around Feste and share the hugs as they used to, life would be perfect. Meanwhile, Neil talks to horses and, it seems, to everything else he encounters. Neil hopes someday to teach people how to use intuitive communication to ride horses — something that Feste predicted Neil would do later in his life.

Pamela and I had a similar dream when we were growing up. We both wanted to learn several languages and be able to create cross-cultural understanding. We both now see that intuitive communication is the ultimate realization of this dream. Pamela said that she once thought learning to talk to animals was the culmination of her heart's desire. But now, as her communication with animals is becoming easier, she is aware that going further, to do what she can to help animals and the earth, is what is truly important.

Suggested Practice

This exercise is designed to give you insight into a past crisis with an animal. Try it using automatic writing, a technique used by authors to move past writers' block. The idea is to begin writing on a topic or start off with a phrase and then, for an assigned period of time, continue to write without stopping — without letting your pen stop moving or leave the paper until the time is up, even if you find yourself writing the same words over and over.

To apply this technique to the exercise, first think back to a crisis you had with an animal. Then ask yourself the following questions and write a page or so in response to each one using the automatic-writing technique.

- Did you sense a heightened intuitive ability at the time of the crisis with your animal?

- Did you form or strengthen an intuitive bond with your animal because of the crisis?

- Did this experience shift the course of your life in any way?

- What did you learn from your animal and from the experience?

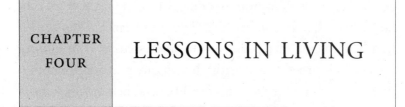

CHAPTER FOUR	LESSONS IN LIVING

*C*onnecting with animals and nature brings you back to what is important in life: staying in touch with your emotions, trusting your inner convictions, and slowing down enough to enjoy life. The stories in this chapter are about learning those lessons in living.

Every animal in your life teaches you something important. And every animal offers you unconditional love. Psychologist and empathy expert Margot Lasher says that animals never disconnect from their true emotions or from what is happening in the moment.[1] They are usually completely genuine and willing to love us unconditionally. Their primary gift and lesson is to help us cultivate these qualities in ourselves.

Animals offer many other lessons too. My horse, Dylan, led me to discover TTEAM and Parelli Natural Horsemanship, two forms of natural horsemanship techniques that I used to overcome his spookiness and stubborn behavior.[2] These techniques also helped me with my fears of riding, which in turn gave me confidence in other areas of my life. Because Dylan has had serious health problems that could not be addressed by conventional medicine, I turned to alternative health care practices for horses, such as the natural trim for his feet.[3] Beyond helping my horse, I needed to learn these things so that I could share what worked for me with clients who have similar problems with their horses. The same is true for my dogs and cats; they taught me how best to help them so that I could share that knowledge with others.

It was a common ancient belief that everything in nature had wisdom to offer, as Dianne Skafte describes in her well-researched book, *When Oracles Speak: Understanding the Signs and Symbols All Around Us*.[4] She relates how premodern humans looked to bees and crows for omens and advice. She tells about an ancient oak tree in Greece, revered for its wisdom, that was visited daily by people coming to seek its counsel. This is a far different view of nature from the one we have, but it has been around a lot longer. For all the mess we've made of the world, perhaps it is time for us to turn again to nature for guidance.

ANNIE

I learned of Annie from my client Martha Siemonsma. Until she got Annie, Martha had never ridden a horse except at dude ranches. She'd always wanted her own horse, but her husband had lobbied against it. After fifteen years of marriage, she finally convinced him to relent. For 350 dollars, she bought Annie, a thirteen-year-old mare of unknown breeding who was being retired from ranch work. Annie would not have been considered an attractive horse, but Martha was told she had been ridden a lot and did not buck, kick, or bite. Martha thought everything would be easy.

Annie and Martha

Annie turned out to be difficult to catch and harder to bridle: she wouldn't stand to be mounted, she was high headed, low backed, and head shy, and she wouldn't allow anyone to pick up her feet. In fact, she kicked anyone who tried. Martha later found out that Annie had been beaten, so her poor behavior made sense. In self-defense, Martha took basic horse-handling and riding lessons from a local woman, but the lessons ended when the woman was injured in an unrelated accident and stopped teaching. After that Martha was on her own. The closest riding instructor, two hours away, didn't take beginners. Martha rode Annie almost every weekend, at a walk and trot only, for their first three years together. She tried to canter but could not slow, stop, or turn Annie. Since she did not have any safe place to practice, she decided she really didn't need to canter anyway.

Things were going fairly well until one day in late summer when Martha was out riding Annie about a mile from home. She started having problems with Annie and decided to return. But for some reason, Annie got spooked and started bucking. Martha was catapulted off, and Annie lost her balance and fell on top of her. Then Annie got up and ran off.

Martha was stunned, injured, scared, alone, and a mile from home. She managed to make it to a water trough in the shade. She had to wait two hours before her husband, worried about her absence, finally found her, and she ended up in the hospital with multiple fractures to her pelvis. Her doctor said she should not even attempt to ride again for a year.

When she was finally able to get out of bed to visit Annie, Martha had to use a walker. She verbally spoke to Annie and told her she knew it was an accident and didn't blame her. She told her how much she loved her and explained that Annie would have to be careful now, because Martha could not move very quickly and could easily be reinjured. She knew Annie understood, because after that, whenever she went into Annie's stall, the horse practically froze in place. She wouldn't even bump Martha with her nose, which was something she had liked to do.

During her convalescence, Martha used natural horsemanship techniques to work with Annie on the ground. She never rode

Annie again; she was just too scared. Annie was getting older and had developed some arthritis, and Martha got the impression that Annie didn't care much for riding either, so they mutually decided that it wasn't necessary; there were plenty of other ways to enjoy each other's company. They both loved taking long walks to go bird watching. Annie carried Martha's bird books, binoculars, camera, water, and lunch for both of them. On these excursions, Martha never needed a lead rope; once off the road she took the rope off, and Annie followed her everywhere.

Martha communicated with Annie by hand signals. She also taught Annie games: going backward through a pole maze, free lunging in a pasture, lowering her head on hand cue, stepping through tires, ground tying, coming when called, standing for bathing, and turning and facing on cue. Through her devotion and gentleness, Annie taught Martha that true beauty has nothing to do with exterior appearances and that even a thousand-pound horse can be controlled with nothing more than a thought, a hand signal, or the strength of a little finger. She also taught Martha the power of love and friendship. Right after the death of her father, Martha went to see Annie. She cried and talked to Annie about her father. As she spoke she felt Annie's nose press into the small of her back, and Annie started massaging her back with her lips. Annie then moved her head in front of Martha and bent her neck so that Martha was pushed up against the horse's body. It seemed to be Annie's idea of how to hug a human. Martha knew that Annie sensed her grief and was trying to comfort her.

When Annie died about a year after that, Martha felt an emptiness that she was certain would never go away. A few months later, however, something happened that made her realize that even death could not separate her from Annie. It was on

a particularly nasty day. The temperature hovered in the low for-
ties with a drizzling rain. Martha was feeling about as gloomy
as the weather and claustrophobic from having been inside too
much. She decided to bundle up and take a long walk. She went
down the road and into a field that she and Annie had loved to
visit. All the memories of the good times they had had together
flooded back, and she could not help but start to cry.

Then the strangest thing happened. She felt warm air on
her face, even though the air was very cold, and she started feeling heavy, as if she couldn't lift her arms. Her whole body
warmed up, as if she were being wrapped in a cocoon. She felt
an intense sense of well-being, relaxation, and comfort, which
lasted for about five minutes. Then she got the sensation that
there was another "presence" in the field with her. At first she
was alarmed, but she quickly received a vivid mental image of a
bay horse. It was Annie. Her tears turned to ones of happiness,
and she wanted to stay in that field forever. But as suddenly
as Annie had come, she left, and nothing remained but the cold.
Annie had visited in spirit to tell Martha that the two of them
would never be apart.

THE ROAD LESS TRAVELED

Because of a trauma she experienced as a young child, Gwen
Orro turned away from people and found solace and companionship in nature instead. Though able to speak, she hardly
said a word until she was eight, but she does recall talking
silently to the flowers and trees when she was young. In her book
Your Sixth Sense, psychologist Belleruth Naparstek identifies
childhood trauma as one of the conditions that can lead to

increased intuitive ability.[5] Gwen developed the ability to communicate intuitively with the natural world, and she carried it into her adult life.

Gwen and Lucky

Gwen contacted me after reading an article about me in the newspaper. She was excited to find someone who openly admitted talking to nature. Now in her seventies, she still communicates with the trees in her yard and with her golden retriever, Lucky, and she still considers herself to be an outsider and an unusual person. It was a revelation to her to learn that more and more people are doing what she has done all her life.

Gwen grew up in Chicago in a black Christian neighborhood. Even though her great-grandfather had founded the
Southern Baptist Church there, Gwen ended up feeling estranged
from her community. Her parents were not big churchgoers, but
her grandfather insisted that she and her sister attend Sunday
school. Gwen told me she found the stories they taught unreal,
like fairy tales. She was indignant when they told her that the
stories were true, and she concluded that the adults at the school
were lying to her. She and her sister decided to skip Sunday
school and go to the lake every Sunday instead.

This experience started what turned out to be a lifetime of
alienation from the black Christian community. Gwen told me
she believes that African slaves were brainwashed by slavery and
that adopting the Christian religion was part of that process. She
thinks primitive African culture was much more nature based. I
would agree.

Chicago is a beautiful city, full of many trees, public parks,
and forest preserves. During her visits to the lake, Gwen really
began to connect with nature. Being outdoors along the beautiful shoreline and parks of Lake Michigan in downtown Chicago
was like paradise and made her feel secure. Gwen says she even
talked to the water, and she remembers two trees that she used
to sit with and talk to as if they were old friends. Her parents
would not let her have a dog, so she connected instead with
what was available to her: trees, birds, flowers, and the lake. She
kept her communications secret from everyone.

In listening to Gwen's story I was struck by the similarity
of her childhood with that of George Washington Carver, the
nineteenth- and twentieth-century botanical genius born in
the 1800s. He too was a loner, who wandered the countryside
when he was young, communing with plants. Carver became
famous for inventing hundreds of new products from plants. To

the consternation of the public, he always attributed his success to the plants, whom he claimed talked to him, telling him how they could be used. Gwen had similar experiences of being considered odd for her beliefs and mannerisms, but she managed to retain her connection with nature into adulthood.

Gwen always had an interest in plants and included botany in her college course work. Later, as an elementary school teacher for children with emotional difficulties, she sought to include botany in their curriculum, but the administration frowned upon it. Frustrated with the confines of that system, she was eventually guided by her communication with nature to move to California. She traveled for a visit and ended up finding a job almost immediately designing and administering a health program for a Native American clinic. When she moved to Northern California, she found a social environment much more to her liking. She still turns to her trees whenever she is depressed, and she understands — better than anyone I know — the capacity of nature to heal, help, and support us if we just ask.

FINDING KISS

I'm sure many people will relate with the following story, which is about ignoring the persistent messages of one's intuition and failing to recognize the intuitive messages that come from an animal. Suzanne Martin came to California from Texas a few years ago to study with me. She continues to practice intuitive communication and has also studied natural horsemanship training. Her skill in both disciplines helped her turn her spooky, high-strung mare, Gabby, into a reliable trail horse who can now be ridden bareback with just a rope halter.

In March 2002, Suzanne began searching for a young horse

to train using natural methods. She found one on the Internet who matched her requirements: "Kiss, an untrained, two-year-old Dutch Warmblood–Thoroughbred cross." From the photographs, Suzanne could tell Kiss was the horse she had been searching for. However, her logical brain stepped in, telling her not to rush things, and suggesting that a better horse might turn up, which squelched her impulse to buy Kiss on the spot.

Suzanne and Kiss

Seven months later, after continuing to look sporadically, she finally realized she had to make a decision or she would go on looking forever. She went back online and found that Kiss was still for sale. The owner, though, was getting ready to sell Kiss at auction. Suzanne went to meet Kiss, who turned out to be even more perfect in person. But just as she was poised to buy Kiss, her logical brain again interfered. Instead of listening to her intuition, Suzanne decided to wait and ponder the purchase. The owner gave her one week to decide.

During that week, she trudged around dutifully looking at other horses, until she finally realized that Kiss was the horse she was meant to have. She'd known that from the minute she'd first seen the picture of Kiss on the Internet. She called the owner and bought Kiss that day.

Suzanne trained Kiss to tolerate a saddle and then lay across her back to prepare her for riding. Intuitively, she felt that it would be safe for her to ride Kiss, but again she let her intellect take over and began to fear that she might get injured if Kiss bucked her off. Even though she had an uneasy feeling about it, she decided to send Kiss to a trainer. The first trainer got into fights with Kiss. Suzanne sent Kiss to a second trainer, with whom Kiss became noticeably depressed. Suzanne realized that it was going to be up to her to ride Kiss and teach her to enjoy having someone on her back. She and Kiss had a great relationship on the ground, so why couldn't Suzanne allow herself to trust Kiss under saddle?

Suzanne rode Kiss bareback at first, and only at a walk. She kept her mind clear of any thought other than a peaceful walk, and that is exactly what she got. Kiss was quiet and willing. Soon she added the saddle, and again Kiss did well. The first time she ever trotted Kiss, she kept a clear picture of a peaceful experience in her mind, and that's what she got. The first time she asked Kiss to canter, she pictured the canter in her mind and everything went perfectly.

Soon Suzanne was ready to take Kiss to her first horse show. Her goal was to expose Kiss to the other horses, ride her around the show grounds, and possibly enter a few competitions. Kiss did well. She remained calm and focused. Suzanne intuitively sent Kiss calming thoughts and pictures of what to do. Kiss sent back messages that everything was fine. That weekend Kiss received two second-place ribbons and one third-place ribbon. Suzanne is convinced that Kiss came into her life to help her learn once and for all to trust her intuition and never again let fear or logic override it.

HAPPY FEET

Can you imagine spending seven months out in nature, hiking and sleeping on the ground? That's how long it took Rachel Pelletier in 2001 to hike the Appalachian Trail from Georgia to Maine, where she lives. I met Rachel when she was in California to visit relatives and attended one of my animal communication workshops. In the workshop the group got on to the subject of communicating with wildlife, and Rachel told us about some of her experiences while hiking the Appalachian Trail.

Hiking from Georgia to Maine is impressive in itself. Rachel's experiences of connecting with nature along the way were fascinating. Rachel was a "through hiker," someone who hikes through from the beginning to the end of the trail. According to tradition, everyone on the trail chooses or is given a trail name. Rachel chose the name Happy Feet. A massage therapist by trade, Rachel performed foot reflexology on herself throughout the hike and managed to avoid developing sore feet. She gave foot massages to other through hikers as well, at shelters along the trail.

Rachel hiking the Appalachian Trail

Rachel met a lot of wildlife along the trail, including bears. She said she could feel an animal's presence before she saw it and knew whether it was a bear, a fox, a moose, or a snake (although, Rachel said, the bears often gave themselves away first by their musty, swampy odor). This ability to feel the presence of an animal grew stronger and surer the longer she was on the trail. Grouse were the only animals who consistently took her by surprise.

When Rachel encountered an animal, she would talk to it in her head or aloud, saying hello and sometimes explaining that she was afraid. She would ask the animal to keep its distance or leave the trail, and the animal usually complied. Though she's not too afraid of bears, Rachel did have a fear of snakes and always asked them to get off the path when she encountered them. As they complied with her request, she would thank them and comment on how beautiful they looked or say how kind they were. She always thanked them for showing themselves.

Rachel said that while she was on the trail those seven months, nothing distracted her from her experience of nature, and she found her connection to nature growing deeper and deeper. She developed a heightened awareness for everything in the environment. She even felt an essence of life from boulders and rock formations. And wherever she needed it while walking the trail, there was a tree to hold on to, to help her over the steep and high places that she feared. It almost seemed as if certain trees were there to help hikers along the trail.

Just as I was absorbing the feeling of this momentous communion with nature that Rachel was describing, she casually mentioned that she had also met her husband-to-be on the trail, and that they were going to be married soon. Rachel had met this man, whose trail name was Tumbleweed, at the beginning of the hike, and they continued to bump into each other every now and then along the trail. Rachel said the experience seemed more than accidental; a marathon and century runner, Tumbleweed could hike much faster than she and had expected to finish the trail in two months. One day they ended up hiking a segment together; the day was perfect, and the rest is history. He slowed down to her pace and took seven months to finish the hike instead of the two he had allotted.

The only civilization that surfaced amid this otherwise idyllic existence, on a somewhat regular basis, were the couple's forays to vending machines in state parks. Rachel said hikers are always hungry on the trail, especially for junk food. One day as they were hiking, a mink started to follow them. It kept pace with Rachel as if it wanted to be with her. She and Tumbleweed detoured toward a state park to check for vending machines, and when they got to the paved road, the mink was still following. Rachel tried to scare it away by yelling and waving, but the mink looked incredibly sad and would not leave. She stopped, calmed herself, and explained to the mink that it had to turn back because of cars and traffic. She could not take it with her; it must return to the woods, where it would be safe. After that talk, the mink quietly turned around and disappeared.

Even though she and Tumbleweed spent months together on the trail, they did not make any plans to see each other again after they reached the trail's end in Maine. They went back home to their own lives. But within two weeks they realized that they had to be together, and he came to live with her in Maine.

A family of loons lives in the pond by their home. They go to sleep hearing the loons call and wake up to the loons at sunrise. The day before their wedding, in 2004, an eagle flew overhead and a snake came to visit. Rachel thanked the animals for visiting, asked the snake to keep its distance, and chatted with it for a while. Many through hikers attended the wedding, which took place on the shores of the loon pond. After sunset, the eighty-foot pine trees around their house swayed in the wind, sounding like an orchestra playing for them.

Rachel's experience on the trail helped her to regain a connectedness to nature that few modern humans can comprehend. Being immersed in nature can bring us back to the knowledge that humans had when they were wild, knowledge that still resides with wild animals and in wild places. Knowledge that is there waiting for us if we choose to seek it.

Suggested Practice

Think about the animals in your past. Recall the experiences with each animal and ask yourself what lesson(s) each one taught you.

Ask your current animals to show you very clearly what lesson(s) they are here to teach you. Thank them for helping you.

On a regular basis, with no distractions, spend some time in nature. Connect again with the pace and feel of the natural world. Observe some animals, wild or domesticated, and study how they manage to fully experience and enjoy the moment. Ask for teaching from the animals and nature. Pay attention to what comes your way.

CHAPTER FIVE	TRANSFORMATIONS

A single event can transform your life, your thinking, and your worldview. The realization that I could actually converse mentally with animals changed my perception of science and the laws of nature. It revolutionized my thinking and took my life in a whole new direction. In this chapter I tell stories of the transforming experiences people have had when connecting and communicating with animals and nature, starting with a story of my own.

DAISY

I've found many uses for my ability in intuitive communication, but none more profound than being able to talk to an animal who is dying. Knowing what an animal wants in this situation has transformed the experience of death for me.

Daisy was a black Labrador. After she was diagnosed with liver cancer, I told her that she could stay with me as long as she wanted, but I would let her go when she was ready. All she had to do was tell me. She seemed almost normal for many months. Then she started suffering incontinence. One morning shortly after that, I woke up and found her with all four legs splayed out, unable to rise. I tried to help her up without success. Then I stopped and asked the question, "Daisy, is it time to go?"

Instantly I heard her answer, "Yes, it's time."

I had no uncertainty or hesitation. I knew beyond doubt that she was ready to leave this life. I took her to the veterinarian and had her put down. She went quickly and easily. Usually, people are very uncertain about making the decision to euthanize, and I was no exception. But developing the ability to communicate with animals eliminated that doubt from my life forever. I felt awful for months after Daisy's death, but it was not because of guilt or distress about my decision. I just had a hard time facing life without my loving Daisy Dogger.

SEEING IS BELIEVING

One spring, when I taught intuitive communication workshops in the Netherlands, I had my students practice interviewing four Norwegian fjord horses at a nearby children's farm. The only information we were given about the horses was that they were all female; we could see that one was young and that one of the adults was pregnant. The students mentally spoke with the horses and then got verification of the responses by questioning the woman who tended the horses.

I could tell this woman was skeptical, but as the students asked her their verification questions, her face opened in amazement. One student asked, "Was that mare over there recently brought in from another farm? Did they use her for jumping and then get rid of her because they wanted a bigger horse?" The astonished caretaker nodded yes.

Another asked, "When they got rid of her, did they get a big black Friesian horse instead? Because that's the image the mare showed me." Again the caretaker nodded.

More questions followed: "Were the other three horses all born here? Is that mare over there the mother of this baby, and is the mare right next to the baby her grandmother? Because that's what the baby said." The caretaker confirmed this too.

In fact, most of the information the students got from the horses turned out to be accurate. One of the students even had an intuitive hunch that Taiga, the pregnant mare, would have a male foal, which proved to be accurate (he was named Albin).

Taiga and her two-day-old colt, Albin

Clearly, the students were not just making clever guesses. The caretaker was so impressed by what she had seen and heard that she immediately wanted to know how she could learn to do what we were doing with the horses. My workshops were over for that spring, but she was thrilled to be able to buy my book and start studying on her own.

THE CHRISTMAS TREE

After reading my book *Learning Their Language*, Annie Traver wrote to tell me that she realized she had been communicating intuitively all her life but had been unaware of it. She recounted an incident that occurred fifteen years before when she went to a Christmas-tree farm with her fiancé and his family. Cutting a live tree was a tradition for his family, but her family had always had synthetic trees, so she had never done it before. When she entered the farm that cold, still evening, she was overcome by a feeling of terror and fear. She looked around and saw fathers and sons, chainsaws in hand, racing to cut down their chosen trees. She realized the feelings were being transmitted to her by the trees, as she had been feeling perfectly fine before walking into the tree farm. She reached out to stroke a small tree, and before she could stop herself she blurted out, "It's trembling." She had actually felt the sensation of trembling, as one might feel when touching a frightened animal. Her fiancé looked at her as if she were insane. She decided right then that cutting a tree was one tradition that would be short lived. She went along with the process that night, but she vowed never to go after a live Christmas tree again. As it turned out, the marriage was short lived too.

My book jogged Annie's memory of the many times she'd had an intuitive communication with an animal. Finally accepting this ability in herself has transformed her life. She now uses her ability every day. She feels more in tune with and sensitive to nature, but she realizes she's really just giving credit to feelings she had, in the past, simply dismissed.

THE BEAVERS

Artist Lori Preusch also read *Learning Their Language* and found that it helped her begin communicating with animals on her own.[1] Lori was already convinced that animals are more intelligent than commonly accepted because of the behavior of the family of beavers living near her house. When Lori's neighbors started shooting the beavers, who for ten years had been destroying trees in the area to make their dams, Lori intervened on their behalf, got the authorities involved, and managed to put a stop to the killing. After that, the beavers abandoned their dam building on her property and dug a twenty-five-foot tunnel about a foot in diameter that diverted water around one of their dams and into the neighborhood lake. For the first time in many years, the lake was full of water all winter long.

Recognizing this behavior as the beavers' way of saying thanks, Lori began to actively seek other connections with the natural world. Her family saved a young Canada goose, seen on the next page in the picture with Lori, who bonded with them. Though it was released to the wild, the goose returned to the family later in life when it was ill and in need of help.

Lori with the Canada goose she rescued

Lori's main interest is in communicating with wildlife and nature, which can be difficult to verify. I do believe it is possible to communicate with anything that is living, and in chapter 1, I cited the credible experimentation that has been done on the reactive capability of plants. But definitive experiments to prove that all of nature has consciousness have yet to be conducted.

In my intuitive conversations with wildlife and nature I have noted a tendency toward a more expanded philosophical quality in the exchange. This is also evident in the following excerpts Lori sent me from the journal she is keeping of her communication with nature:

OLD TREE

I would like you to consider telling the world what it is like to be a tree. . . . I am in deep need of love. More than you would imagine. Standing tall for the world to see a wide trunk and great spanning branches, leaves me virtually unnoticed as a being. . . . Few think to give love to one that appears so static. . . . My leaves, however, and my branches and buds and flowers are every bit as alive as you. But because the years have silenced your ability to hear, I am dismissed completely. . . . You, my dear, have found your voice. You will be changing now because of it. I thank you for your deep, heartfelt consideration. Please speak with me often. I would love the connection and to begin teaching you more about us. If only you sought to seek my wisdom and find your long forgotten language. . . . I will share my love and wisdom without any bounds.

SAN JUAN RIVER

Flow like the river. . . touch all that you meet with a gentle embrace. . . . Do not be troubled by others. . . . Yours is not of theirs, just as my flow is not part of another river's. Follow your own wisdom . . . know who you are and where you are going, like a river. Let the sun shine on your surface, reflecting love back to the world. Don't be troubled by the storms, they can never stop your flow. Just move around them. Just move around.

Lori is opening up more and more to her intuitive side. She is taking classes in intuition and now sees how much her life has changed since the beavers set her on what she describes as her "right path."

SOLSTICE

It's always amazing to me to see how one small intuitive interaction between a human and another species, like the one in this story, can have such a significant effect.

Solstice, a gray, Warmblood-Thoroughbred cross who shares a barn with my horse, Dylan, is an especially large horse. He has been trained in natural horsemanship and is a complete gentleman, but if you don't know that, he can be intimidating. I often take students to the stable to work with the horses, and it's always interesting to see their reaction to him. Usually, they start out thinking he is tough and overpowering. But when they talk to him they discover he is actually very sweet. All I ever have to do to discourage him from doing something I don't want is to wag a finger at him or raise my voice slightly. Once I yelled at him rather severely when he was about to kick one of my dogs, and he looked truly shocked and concerned that I was angry.

When Trisha McCagh, an animal communicator from Australia, visited me one summer, we went to the stable to work with the horses. Though familiar with horses as a child, she had not had much to do with them since and in fact was a bit apprehensive around them. When we got to the stable, the horses were up in the pasture, so I sent Trisha to find them and to try some communication exercises with Solstice. I told her the horses were older and fairly sedate, but, aware of her lack of familiarity with horses, I advised her to keep her distance. I set about cleaning the paddocks and about a half hour later went to

Trisha and Solstice

find them. She and Solstice were on top of the hill standing side-by-side, obviously deep in conversation.

Trisha said when she found Solstice she sat down on the opposite end of the pasture from him, intending to observe and converse with him at a distance. But Solstice had other ideas. He grazed his way over to where she was sitting, making her very nervous about being on the ground with his huge feet so close. She kept hearing him say, "I won't hurt you. I won't hurt you. Don't be afraid." She stood up and started to pat him. She found it felt completely safe to stand close to him and communicate intuitively, which is what they ended up doing for the next half hour.

In that one encounter, Trisha lost her apprehension and was transported back to her childhood love and trust of horses. Later, my horse Dylan gave her a ride around the apple orchard. Trisha is now planning to get back into riding horses.

RAVEN HILL

When Nancy Hensley and her partner began building a new home on a property in rural Northern California, windows bloodied by dive-bombing ravens were not part of their dream. But that became the major feature of the landscape that spring. It was mating season, and the ravens were especially vigilant: they were dive-bombing the house's windows to attack the images of unwelcome rival ravens they saw reflected there. I have had songbirds do this to my windows, but never anything as large as a raven. When a raven attacks its own reflection in a window, it severely harms itself. The situation was getting gruesome, and Nancy had already tried using reflective mylar, noise-makers, and hawk silhouettes in the window to no avail. The builders were so annoyed that they wanted to shoot the ravens.[2] Nancy's partner was at the point of agreeing to that when Nancy called on me for help. She hoped that there was another way to stop the raven attacks.

Although I tried, I was unable to influence the ravens' behavior or diminish their aggression. I urged Nancy to begin talking with the ravens every day about the problem, find ways to honor and appease the ravens, and get the humans to back off for a while. She followed my advice, and one night a few weeks later, she went to her unfinished house and sat alone in one of the rooms. She lit a candle and tried to talk to the ravens. She closed her eyes and in her imagination was transported into a raven's nest. She felt herself get very small until she was the size of a newly hatched raven. Then she imagined the father raven flying up and landing on the edge of the nest. He was *huge*. He made it very clear that it was his job to protect his offspring and *nothing* would stand in his way. He had no more to say. Nancy opened her eyes and thought, "Well, that isn't very profound." She was hoping for something more significant or deep from the communication.

Then her mind wandered and she thought to herself, "These ravens can't be as smart as people say if they think they see other ravens in the windows — pretty stupid really." She sat a little while longer and then got up to leave. With her candle in hand she turned and practically jumped out of her skin. She had seen someone over her shoulder. Then she realized it was just her own reflection in the window. Of course! That was what the ravens were trying to tell her. To them, the ravens they saw reflected in the windows posed a threat to their chicks. They could not ignore those strange ravens no matter what Nancy said or did.

Nancy found it a humbling experience to finally realize what was going on. She felt self-centered to have expected the ravens to do as she asked. Why should they obey her wishes when their chicks were in danger? She was sure the ravens had heard her talking to them each day and had appreciated the contact, but she now realized that they had to do what they thought was right. They couldn't make a deal with her just because she asked for it.

After that, Nancy started reading about raven biology and mythology. Ravens started to show up everywhere in her life, and she and her partner found that they looked forward to this contact. Nancy put more reflection-blocking material on the windows and the dive-bombing decreased. She and her partner named their property Raven's Hill and built an altar to honor the ravens. Nancy kept a journal of her daily talks with the ravens and found they were becoming a significant part of her life. She and her partner enjoyed watching the ravens play on the wind currents, and they spent hours in late spring observing the babies learn how to fly. The whole raven family would sit in the top of an old snag, and one at a time, the juveniles would take off, executing flips and dives. You could almost hear the others applauding as each youngster landed.

Nancy in her garden at Raven's Hill

At last report, the ravens weren't attacking the house much anymore, and the humans and ravens at Raven's Hill were living in reasonable harmony. Perhaps once a month there will be a tap or two on the windows. During the nesting season the tapping increases, but only for a few weeks. Nancy said the ravens have taught her to listen to herself. She didn't need to seek outside for an answer to her problem with the ravens; she had only to pay attention to the wisdom that came from her own intuition.

LOST IN CALHOUN COUNTY

This story is really about the transformation of a whole town through its connection with one large dog. It started when Cathy Smith stopped in for the evening at the Best Western in Oxford, Calhoun County, Alabama. She and her dogs Ellie, a corgi, and Gavin, an Irish wolfhound, were on their way home from the Westminster Kennel Club Dog Show in New York. When she loaded the dogs in the van the next morning, Gavin managed to push a control that opened the back door. He and Ellie jumped out of the van and rushed through the open door of another guest's room. The man in the room was terrified and yelled at them. Gavin panicked, ran off at top speed, and soon disappeared from sight.

Cathy searched throughout the town but could not find Gavin. She called me in desperation. When I tuned in intuitively to Gavin I saw images of a church and a wooded area with a dump. I felt that Gavin was traveling and I could not convince him to slow down. Cathy knew exactly the spot I was describing. She found fresh Gavin tracks there but could not catch up with him.

She went back to her home in Lubbock, Texas, leaving the search temporarily to Chirlee Brown and some other people in Oxford who had volunteered to help. The police got involved, and several stories appeared in the local newspaper, but no one could find Gavin. After about a week, Cathy asked me to check again. This time I felt Gavin had gone into a forest above town. Cathy drove back to Oxford and found the area but was warned that the people in the hills guarded their privacy and would likely shoot at anyone who came on their property. She didn't know what to do. As she stood looking up at the hills a man came walking down and said, "Are you the lady who lost her dog? I'll help you look for him." He organized a crew of searchers who found Gavin's tracks in the hills but were unable to find Gavin.

Another week passed and Cathy called me again. When I talked to Gavin this time, I saw him running with deer in a wooded area with lots of water. I told her to travel more to the east and described some other features of the landscape. Shortly after we talked, a woman called Cathy to report that she had spotted Gavin running in that area. They found fresh tracks, but no Gavin. He was lost somewhere amid hundreds of acres of woods and creeks. Cathy called in a professional tracker, but that proved unsuccessful too. Chirlee and a group of dedicated volunteers kept up the search.

Cathy called me again in the seventh week of the search. This time I saw Gavin in a triangular piece of land bordered on three sides by water, in a sort of cave area at the base of a cliff. Chirlee knew exactly what I was describing: an expanse of land bordered on two sides by creeks and on one side by a lake. When she and Cathy got there they found Gavin's tracks were everywhere, but they still could not locate the dog.

Some of the searchers had gone from being skeptical about Cathy using an animal communicator to being convinced that I was tracking Gavin quite accurately. They took my information seriously now, realizing something they had thought was a joke was actually quite real. What was frustrating for everyone was that even though Gavin had been located he was purposely avoiding human contact.

Cathy had to return to work in Texas. The volunteer searchers decided to try to trap Gavin. A welder in town fashioned a live trap big enough to hold an Irish wolfhound. Acting on a tip that Gavin had been spotted at an old barn in the area, the searchers set the trap there. Two hours later Gavin went into the trap, seven weeks from the day he first ran off.

Gavin at Chirlee's the night he was found

At the veterinary clinic five hundred ticks were removed from his body. He had lost about eighty pounds, half his body weight. His hair was thin, he had cuts and wounds all over, and he had been shot, though the wound was not serious. Gavin was treated and released to Chirlee. Cathy arrived the next day to reunite with the dog she just could not give up on.

Gavin gained back all his weight and much of his hair and even entered a few dog shows in Texas. But Cathy discovered that during his ordeal, Gavin had contracted an internal parasite, which had invaded his lungs. He finally succumbed to a weakened immune system and died about nine months after he had been found. Cathy still gets calls about Gavin. The good people of Oxford, Alabama will not soon forget him, or the fact that intuitive communication — something considered to be impossible — was what helped rescuers to find him.

Gavin with rescuers

Suggested Practice

Ask for transformation of some aspect of your life. Talk out loud to an animal and ask for help in resolving a problem and finding new solutions. Find a place in nature that you like being in. Sit there quietly and ask for guidance directly from the spirit of that place. Now pay attention to anything that happens around you and to any feelings, ideas, or impressions that come to you. Jot everything down. Stay aware over the next few days and weeks for messages and experiences of transformation.

CHAPTER SIX	PRACTICAL MAGIC

My riding instructor, Michelle Tobin, told me of an experience she'd had during a lesson. She was about to give the student an instruction when the horse completed the task before she'd said a word. All of sudden it occurred to her that this had been happening for some time, in all her lessons. She realized that the horses were hearing her thoughts, seeing her mental images, and then anticipating her verbal instructions before she gave them.

Looking at my horse, Dylan, she said, "So it would be as if I were to *think* a command to Dylan..." and as she spoke, Dylan stepped sideways with his hind legs. Michelle said, "See what I mean? Just like that. I was thinking and imagining that he should do that!" I said, "I know. They understand us totally. That's what I keep telling people." Then to Dylan I said, "Horses are a lot smarter than people think, aren't they, Dylan?"

In response, Dylan nodded his head up and down about five times. He only nods when I have food, when he's playing with other horses, or when I say something he really agrees with.

Everywhere I go, people tell me stories about how their animals have heard and understood them. It no longer surprises me. Animals are experts at intuitive communication. They understand everything we say, think, feel, or visualize. Unfortunately that means you can't hide anything from them, and it's useless to try. However, you can use their ability to your benefit when it comes to training, as the stories in this chapter demonstrate.

THE PHOEBMONSTER

For a long time I wanted to get a kitten but resisted because I already had two dogs and two cats. What's more, I felt sure my oldest cat would not appreciate a kitten. But I met a kitten I couldn't resist, so I brought her home. I was hoping she would eventually play with Tule, my two-year-old cat, who wanted a friend and who would occasionally ambush Hazel, my twenty-one-year-old cat, in a futile attempt to engage her. I also hoped the new kitty would get along well with Hazel or, barring that, would respect her and give her a wide berth. I talked to all the cats, showed them endless mental movies of how I wanted them to behave, and asked them please to get along.

I isolated the kitten for a few weeks and then put them together. They didn't try to kill each other, but they weren't being chummy, either. There was a lot of hissing and horrid behavior. When not refereeing, I would sit quietly and imagine them all lying curled up together or nimbly chasing one another about the house. I even imagined the sound of cats happily running back and forth in play.

Phoebe as a kitten

I really didn't think this kitten experiment was going to work. In my bleaker moments I figured that instead of two cats who disliked and avoided each other, I would have three. But I didn't give enough credit to the intuitive process or factor in the unique character of the new kitten.

I named that kitten Phoebe but soon nicknamed her the Phoebmonster, because she was pushy and had a fearless personality. She wanted the two other cats to be her friends and was not going to give up until she got that. She waded calmly through all kinds of aggressive behavior in pursuit of her goal. By the end of three months all my visions had been realized: All three cats were playing together and chasing one another through the house. They also slept peacefully together on my desk, which made me happy but left me with virtually no space to work. Hazel not only accepted the new kitty, she loved her. It was success beyond my wildest dreams, courtesy of intuitive communication and a radical little cat.

EVERYONE HAS A STORY

The stories people tell about their experiences with intuitive communication — and everyone seems to have one — often center on dealing with bad behavior. For example, on a visit to my chiropractor, two women who work there, Robin Gates and Maggie Wingfield, each had stories to tell. Robin, who trains animals as a hobby, told a story about a Thoroughbred mare, who seemed frightened of everything and could not stand still. The mare belonged to a friend, who finally sent the horse to Robin to train. For the first two weeks, all Robin did was sit quietly with the horse, sending it feelings of love and saying, "I just want to be your friend." Eventually, the horse calmed down, and Robin began riding her. If the horse became tense during riding, Robin stopped, sat quietly, and sent positive messages. The horse responded well to Robin's training. Ultimately the mare became so sedate that children could safely ride her.

Robin had another story about a Jack Russell terrier someone sent to her for training. After trying everything she knew, she had to concede that she could not train the dog. She couldn't even get him to pay any attention to her. He wanted only to play with the other dogs in the house and would have nothing to do with people. Exasperated, Robin said to her husband, "I am going to send that dog back to the owner. He will just have to remain untrained. I am not going to try anymore." At that moment, the dog stopped playing with the other dogs and looked at Robin. Then he came and jumped in her lap. From then on he gave her his undivided attention.

Maggie Wingfield's story was about her cat Lightning, who had been ill. She took him to a holistic practitioner who advised nutritional supplements for the problem. But Maggie could not find a way to disguise the supplements well enough in his food to persuade Lightning to eat them. She tried talking to Lightning, reasoning with him, and offering him bribes. At her wits' end, she sat staring at Lightning and finally said to him, "What am I going to do, Lightning? How can I get you to eat this? You need it to get better." At that moment the image popped into her head of a can of Whiskas, a brand of cat food she had abandoned when she switched to a holistic diet. She bought some Whiskas, and it turned out to be the only food in which Lightning would accept his supplements. Maggie's story is actually about an animal using intuitive communication to train a person, but that happens too!

When I went from the front office into the adjustment room, the first thing my chiropractor, Neal Gates, said to me was, "I have a great story for you about talking to Katie!" Neal had read my book and then tried out the talking techniques with Katie, his Yorkshire terrier. He related that he had talked to her as he held her in his arms and told her out loud that he knew things were difficult because of some new dogs in the household. He explained to her that some of the other dogs had physical problems and needed extra attention. As he spoke, Katie made noises in response as if verbally agreeing, which was not something she normally did. Neal told her how sorry he was that she had to share the limelight as she continued to "talk" to him. Finally he told her that he would try to give her special attention and that he would always love her best. As he said that, Katie closed her eyes and, in an uncharacteristic gesture, laid her head on his heart. Neal's comment to me was, "This stuff really works!"

OLLIE

My sister Anne once called me for advice on how to deal with a behavior problem she was having with her shire cross draft

Ollie and Anne

horse, Ollie. Because of schedule constraints the only time she had to ride him was during the stable horses' normal feeding time, and he was acting up. Ollie is a total food hound, and he was not pleased to have to work when everyone else was eating. I advised Anne to tell Ollie exactly how much time they would spend riding, and to assure him that no one would get his food while they were out. On the days when he had to go through this ordeal, I told her to promise him extra treats. Like magic, that was the end of her problems with Ollie. All she'd done was talk to him about the problem, but it was enough.

Anne also has had success when simply *thinking* a message to Ollie. For example, one day she was riding and some rowdy horses in the arena clearly were making Ollie nervous. Anne sent him the following thoughts: "Ollie, if you just relax, put your ears down, and walk along the fence toward the gate, we will go and get your dinner." He immediately complied, without the need for further physical or verbal cues. Someone standing nearby asked, "What on earth did you just do with your horse?" Anne replied, "We did the Vulcan mind-meld."

JOSE AND FREYA

Gerrie Huits, a student of mine from the Netherlands who now works as a communicator herself, sent me a story about using intuitive communication to facilitate the resolution of aggression between two dogs. A friend came to visit Gerrie to show off her new dog, Jose, a greyhound rescued from the streets in Spain. Gerrie's friend already had two other greyhounds rescued from Spain, and one of them, Freya, was poorly socialized and reserved with people and animals. Freya did not like changes in her routine or her environment, and she was not very happy with Jose. She had even tried to bite him.

Jose and Freya

Fearing a recurrence, Gerrie's friend asked her to communicate intuitively with Jose to counsel him on how to avoid such attacks. Gerrie connected with Jose, who told her he was wise beyond his years. As she talked with Jose, she suddenly felt very sad and then got a mental picture of Freya. She connected intuitively with Freya, who was back at her friend's house. Freya told her that rather than feeling jealous, the puppy was actually making her sad because he represented everything she did not have but longed for: a free and playful spirit, joy at contact with humans and animals, fearlessness, and the courage to love.

Then something odd happened. Gerrie heard Jose start talking mentally to Freya. It was as if Gerrie were a bystander listening in to the dogs' conversation. Jose told Freya that he understood how she was feeling and that he was sympathetic. He told her to try to look at life more positively and suggested that she could learn how to be happier from him. He was willing to help, and regardless of what she decided, he said he would love her.

Gerrie heard Freya respond with surprise, telling Jose she hadn't thought of that possibility and would consider it.

That evening, Gerrie's friend called to report that when she and Jose arrived home, Freya was waiting at the door for them. Instead of growling, Freya gently touched Jose's head with her nose. Shortly thereafter, Freya stopped behaving aggressively and began acting as if she were Jose's mother. She started playing with him and sleeping with him on the couch. When they're out for a walk, she now protects him against big dogs. When Gerrie talked to Freya a few weeks later, Freya said she had learned a lot from Jose. Her new purpose in life was to be his mom, which she said she was enjoying.

CROSS TRAINING

Sarah Reid, another student of mine who is now working on her own as a communicator, has used intuitive communication to train a variety of animals. With Oreo, her mustang, she used the technique to calm him down the first day she got him. He was a nervous wreck after having been rounded up by helicopter, vaccinated, and freeze branded. But when she communicated intuitively with him, his fear subsided. Sarah said Oreo has been an unusual horse to train. He is more like a wild animal than a domestic horse, and he is very responsive to her intuitive messages to him. When out on the trail, he notices the coyotes, deer, and rabbits before any of the other horses do. Rather than spooking at wildlife, though, he just blows air through his nose and stands and watches. To train Oreo all she ever has to do is ask for what she wants using intuitive communication and explain why, and Oreo complies.

Oreo and Sarah

Sarah used intuitive communication to calm an unruly neighborhood dog as well. The dog would wait until his owners left for work, then jump the fence to prowl the neighborhood. He was aggressive toward other dogs and toward people, yet he was not street-smart. Several times, Sarah almost hit him when he ran in front of her car. At around three thirty every afternoon, shortly before his owners returned home, the dog would jump back into his yard.

Sarah decided to try talking to him. She explained that what he was doing was dangerous, that he could get killed by a car or picked up by animal control. He told her that he felt he needed to patrol the street and be protective, to have a presence in the neighborhood. Sarah explained that the street was neutral territory belonging to everyone. She asked if he could instead patrol from behind his own fence. She explained that he could still bark, but he would be safer in his yard. He told her he understood and agreed. In the two years since she had that talk with him, she has seen him out of his yard only twice.

Sarah has even used intuitive communication to change the behavior of mockingbirds. One mockingbird near her home used to begin singing around ten every evening and continue throughout the night, stopping around seven in the morning. He was loud, annoying, and he kept her awake. She tried to shoo him off his favorite tree. She wore earplugs and put a pillow over her head. She tried blasting the bird off his telephone pole with a water hose. Nothing worked.

Finally, in desperation, she tried talking to him. Focusing intently, she sent a blanket message to the neighborhood mockingbirds. She praised them for the variety of their song and acknowledged they were great singers. But, she explained, their singing kept her awake all night. She asked them to move over one block to an empty lot, so their singing wouldn't bother people as much. She also asked that they please not sing at night and that they start no earlier than five thirty in the morning.

The next night there was silence. The mockingbirds had stopped singing. At five thirty the following morning, they started again. She watched the clock for several weeks to verify this. Every morning, the birds started singing almost exactly at five thirty. Clearly they got the message!

CHEETAHS AND PALLAS CATS

Lorike van Helsdingen and her husband work at a private endangered-species breeding zoo in the Netherlands. When one of their charges, Questa, a thirteen-year-old cheetah, had a persistent swelling in her cheek, they called for the veterinarian. In order to prepare Questa for treatment, they had to get her into a shed, so she could be easily guided into a cage and then anesthetized. But Questa refused to go into the shed. Lorike's husband tried for an hour to herd her into the shed, and then he and Lorike tried together, with no luck. Suddenly Lorike, who has attended my workshops, realized she could just talk to Questa. So she explained that the veterinarian was coming to help Questa with the pain in her mouth. Then she said, "If you want to get out of pain, go in the shed." Questa looked at Lorike, then quickly went inside. It turned out she had an infected tooth that had to be pulled.

Lorike and some of the cheetahs

On another occasion, after one of the female cheetahs had mated, Lorike could not tell whether the big cat had become pregnant. After a few weeks, she asked the cheetah, "Can you show me if you have babies inside you?" The cheetah looked at Lorike and then lay down on her side to expose her belly. Lorike saw a movement in the cheetah's flank, and she knew the animal was pregnant.

When a different pregnant cheetah jumped through a glass window in her shelter and cut herself on the glass, Lorike and her husband had to weigh their decision about treatment: if the cheetah needed stitches, the anesthesia would not be good for her or her cubs. Lorike asked the big cat, "What should we do? Do you need the vet or can we wait and see?" The cheetah came forward to show Lorike her cuts. It was obvious they were not too severe. Lorike treated them with a topical antibiotic, the cuts healed, and five weeks later the cheetah delivered four beautiful cubs.

Cats, whether they are big or small, like to dig in the dirt to bury their feces. In part this is a survival instinct to hide their scent. The problem with having cats in captivity is that you must regularly check their stools to monitor their health. This was the case with the small, rare Pallas cats at the breeding zoo. Pallas cats look something like a cross between an Abyssinian and a bobcat. They are quite beautiful, but shy of humans. A pair of Pallas cats had recently had a litter, but all the kittens died of toxoplasmosis. To determine whether the parents were disease carriers, Lorike had to collect and analyze their stools daily. After a few days of crawling through enclosures searching for hidden treasure, Lorike decided to ask for help from the cats. She explained what she was doing and what she needed from them. She told them she was trying to help them have healthy kittens in the future. The next day when she went to their enclosures, the Pallas cats had left their stools right by the door, so Lorike could easily collect them.

Lorike is adept at receiving messages from animals, so she is able to respond to them when they need her help. One day, after cleaning the enclosure of a male cheetah named Nairo, she walked past him and felt a fleeting pain in her right hand. She concluded that Nairo was sending her that pain as a message and he must have had a problem with his right paw, since her hand was perfectly fine. Then she noticed that Nairo would not stand up. When she and her husband examined him, they found inflammation in Nairo's right foot and a badly swollen toe.

A similar exchange happened with the zoo's resident peacock, whom Lorike usually feeds at the same time every morning. But one morning he ran from her rather than coming for the food. She knew that he wanted her to follow him so he could show her something. He led her to some old birdcages, stopped, and stared in. There were two young buzzards trapped in the cages. Once they were released, the peacock went back to his breakfast, very satisfied with himself.

Suggested Practices

A NEW WAY OF TALKING

To use intuitive communication for a training situation, you need to experiment with changing your beliefs and your own behaviors. Try out the new belief that your animal is as intelligent as any person. Speak out loud to your animal just as you would a human and try believing that your animal can comprehend everything you say, just as a person would. Behave as if you believe that your animal can hear your thoughts, feel your feelings, and see the images you form in your mind. Sometimes this simple experiment will result in marked behavioral changes in the animal.

MAKING MOVIES

If you are having a behavioral problem with your animal, discuss it out loud and in detail with the animal. Explain what you want to have happen and why. Then close your eyes and imagine what you want your animal to do. Make a mental movie of exactly how you want your animal to behave. Infuse this visualization with the emotion you would feel if your animal actually behaved as you are imagining. Make the movie feel like a real-life experience by adding in sensory details. When you have finished, say to your animal, "That is my dream of how things could be. If you could do that for me, it would make me really happy." Then see what happens.

If you want your animal to try something new and challenging, demonstrate what you want by letting your animal see another animal performing the new task or by closing your eyes and mentally imagining the new activity for your animal.

Make sure to acknowledge and reward any actions your animal takes that demonstrate that he or she heard and understood your requests.

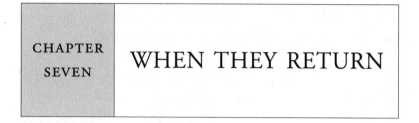

| CHAPTER SEVEN | WHEN THEY RETURN |

The concepts of spirituality and reincarnation in animals are difficult for many people to accept. When I first became involved in the field of intuitive communication, I had no particular beliefs about spirituality or reincarnation. But my experiences in communicating intuitively have convinced me that animals do have spirit and can reincarnate.[1] In this chapter, I share some amazing stories about animals and reincarnation, and give you my best advice on how to recover from the death of an animal.

COPING WITH THE DEATH OF AN ANIMAL

As an animal lover, unless you are especially fond of parrots or desert tortoises, you'll probably outlive many animal companions in your lifetime. I have a favorite quote about that from the book *Separate Lifetimes* by Irving Townsend: "We who choose to surround ourselves with lives even more temporary than our own, live within a fragile circle, easily and often breached."

Many people have told me that going through the death of their animal was more difficult than losing a relative or spouse, and that they felt guilty for grieving so deeply over an animal. I don't see how any of us can avoid such profound feelings, given the nature of the bond we share with our animals. Animals are pure spirits who love us and devote themselves to us without reservation. Not many humans are capable of that. Animals are totally tuned in to us, and once a bond is established, they never abandon us emotionally. When your animal dies you lose all that. You are left with a void that nothing seems to fill.

The question then becomes, How can you cope with the death of an animal? I think that first you must accept the fact that there will be a lot of grief to work through. For me, the only time that isn't true is when the animal is very old and experiences a slow decline. In those situations I am not so sad, but if an animal dies an untimely or unexpected death, it can be very difficult. Unfortunately, the only way to get out of grief is to go through it. It may help to take calming herbs (such as chamomile tea) and calming flower essences (like rescue remedy[2]) throughout the day or use the essential oil of lavender as aromatherapy. I have also used the homeopathic remedy Ignacia amara[3] for grief and found it helpful. These aids are available at health food stores.

Take special care of your body and your emotions when you are grieving. Get massages, take hot tubs and saunas, and get lots of sleep. Rent some funny movies to lift you out of depression, even if only temporarily. Let yourself cry as much as you need to. Some people can be insensitive about the death of an animal, so be careful not to tell people how you feel unless you know they will be supportive. If you have no one to confide in, check with your local humane society to find a therapy group for people who have lost their animals.

You eventually will recover, and you will probably get another animal and go through the same process again. Because we are continually going through this experience, animal lovers are some of the most educated people around when it comes to understanding grief and death.

If yours is a multi-animal household, you may find that your surviving animals will also grieve for the one who died. You can use many of the same remedies for them as for yourself: herbs, essences, massage, and homeopathic medicines. Consult a holistic veterinarian for assistance.4

Often the hardest part of the dying process is deciding whether or not to euthanize an animal. Base your decision on the animal's quality of life. If an animal is in severe pain that can't be alleviated, is unable to move and eliminate normally, or over time has become unable to eat or uninterested in eating, it may be more merciful to help the animal die. Choosing euthanasia is always hard, but I feel that sometimes it is what our animals want us to do for them. In other cases, an animal may be willing to endure a little pain in order to stay with us as long as possible.

KITTY

Sometimes you just know it is the right thing to euthanize an animal, as I did with my black Labrador, Daisy. A student of mine, Virginia Magruder, had a similar experience with her older cat, Kitty. Kitty had spinal damage and a long history of physical struggle and discomfort. For more than a year, Virginia had been asking for a clear message from Kitty if he wanted assistance to leave his body, but she had only felt vague anxiety whenever she contemplated euthanizing him. Kitty's health had begun to deteriorate rapidly, but he was still as alert as ever for attention and love. Then one day, as she was thinking of Kitty, she felt a certainty that he was finished with his body and ready to move on. It was a very physical feeling, she said. Every cell in her body was 100 percent certain. She knew she was hearing Kitty's wishes and could now act on them.

Kitty

When she came home from work that day, Kitty came out of the closet where he had been staying, purred, and wanted to be petted. She knew he was ready to go and wanted to leave in a dignified manner. She made the appointment with Kitty's devoted veterinarian, Todd Czarnecki. At the clinic they set up a room with candles, bright towels, and a sheepskin rug for Kitty to lie on. He left very peacefully, with no struggle. Virginia said that although her husband, Munro, and Dr. Czarnecki were both very upset, she felt only feelings of immense love, peacefulness, and freedom that she knew came from Kitty. She thought of all the animals she had seen die and realized they were all there to help her learn this lesson of letting go. In her email to me she said, "What incredible companions animals are on our journey through this life."

WHAT HAPPENS NEXT?

All the stories that follow concern connecting with animals' spirits after death and through reincarnation. It can be comforting to believe that your animal's spirit can outlast its body, but you do not need to adopt that belief in order to enjoy these stories.[5] They are convincing to me, but I am not presenting them as definitive proof.[6] Mainly, I hope you will find them intriguing and thought provoking, and I suspect you will find that some of the circumstances are not so easy to explain away.

BRYDIE

I will start with my own experience with Brydie, my border collie cross. I got her from the pound when she was five months

old. I had just lost Daisy, my black Labrador, and I wanted a
new friend for my remaining dog and myself. When I got her
home, Brydie took every chance she could to get up behind me,
on the couch or on the bed, and lick my ears. Every time she did
it, my mind flashed back to the memory of putting Maka, my
Australian shepherd, to sleep ten years earlier. After I put Maka
down, I sat in my car outside the veterinary clinic for a few
moments. As I sat there thinking of her, I received an image of
her as a puppy, perched on my shoulder, licking my ears. I
assumed it was her way of saying good-bye and showing me
what she looked like as a puppy, because I had adopted her when
she was older and had never seen her as a puppy. I had completely forgotten about that vision until I brought Brydie home.

Brydie

Brydie continued to lick my ears at every opportunity, until I began to wonder whether she could in fact be Maka, coming back to me. I called one of my colleagues and asked her to ask Brydie about this, since I knew I could not be objective about the subject. My colleague called back to tell me that Brydie said she was indeed my old dog Maka and wanted to know why it had taken me so long to figure it out.

Maka

Here's the clincher. From the moment I set down the phone, Brydie never again repeated that particular behavior.

CISCO

Jeanne Owen met Cisco when she was out shopping for a new horse. The ad sounded perfect: a gentle, gaited paint gelding.

But when she went to see him, he was backed into a corner of an arena, saddled and bridled, and scared to death. She got feelings of anger, defensiveness, and potential violence from him. She looked at him and thought, "This can't be the horse I am supposed to have. He doesn't match my mental picture." When the owner came over, she told him she wasn't interested after all and turned to leave. Then she heard a voice say, "But you don't understand. I'm Danny." Danny was the name of a much loved Welsh pony Jeanne owned as a child. She turned back around and told the owner that on second thought, she'd better take another look.

The owner rode Cisco around the arena and then agreed to let Jeanne ride the horse out on the trail. She had a remarkable ride. They rode for more than an hour, and Cisco was absolutely calm. Jeanne felt totally safe riding him. When she got back to the ranch, the owner greeted her, amazed that she had not had any problems with the horse bucking or rearing. She decided then and there to buy Cisco to save him from this man, and she told the owner she'd take him.

As she walked Cisco to the horse trailer, the owner told her to wait while he got a whip to load the horse into the trailer. When the man left, Jeanne looked at Cisco and told him that if he wanted to go with her he'd better get into the trailer pronto. He walked right in. The owner returned with a whip and stud chain and asked in astonishment, "How did you get him to load?"

"I just asked him nicely," Jeanne replied.

She and Cisco got along famously. After about a week she started to take him on trail rides, and he was perfect. But she was still mystified by the voice she had heard claiming to be Danny. A few weeks after she brought him home she was sitting at a picnic table and Cisco was grazing untethered nearby. She turned

Cisco and Jeanne

to him and said, "So, you really are Danny, huh?" Cisco brought up his head, stopped grazing, and walked over to the picnic table. He stood right at the end of the table and nudged her away with his nose. He put both front feet onto the table as if he were going to get up on it. Then he lowered his nose to the table and waited for Jeanne to react. She laughed and cried simultaneously as she recognized the trick: She and her brother had taught Danny to put his front feet up onto a railing their father had built to separate their yard from the driveway. With his feet up on the railing, they then taught Danny to lower his head between his feet to take a bow. Here was this magnificent horse telling Jeanne, "Okay, here's the proof. Remember this?"

Jeanne said Cisco has shown her over and over that she can trust him. His behavior shows her that he remembers their earlier times together, when she was just a three-year-old girl

learning to ride. She is sure Danny and she have found each
other again, and this time his name is Cisco.

NOW DO YOU KNOW ME?

Getting information intuitively from your own animals can
often be harder than receiving information from an animal you
are unfamiliar with. That's because you already know so much
about your animals that any information you get seems like
something you made up. To get around that, I have devised several exercises for beginners. One of them is called Ask for a
Question. It's a very simple but effective exercise. Instead of asking a question of your animal, ask the animal if he or she has a
question for you. Then answer the question as best you can,
without hesitation.

In a workshop I taught in Chicago I had the class try this
exercise, and then we discussed the results. Several people talked
about how the exercise had led to actual discussions with their
animals, which was, of course, my intent. Then one woman
raised her hand and said that something weird had happened for
her. When she closed her eyes, she saw her current dog. Then
the image switched to a dog she had had five years before,
changed back to her current dog, and shifted again to her previous dog. Then she heard the question, "Now do you know who
I am?"

BOO BOO

One day, Debbie Duval was practicing intuitive communication
on her friend Helen's cats, Darrin and Tabitha. At the end of the

Darrin

practice she asked each cat to tell her something that would convince Helen that she was really communicating with them. From Darrin, she heard the words "Boo Boo" loudly in her head. She said it was so strange that she knew she hadn't made it up, so she wrote it down.

When Debbie spoke with Helen to go over her results, she asked, "First of all, who is 'Boo Boo?' Darrin said very loudly that he wants Boo Boo."

Helen looked puzzled and told Debbie that Boo Boo was the name she and her husband had given an old army blanket (long since discarded) that a previous cat, now deceased, had liked to sleep on. They concluded that Darrin was the former cat returning and wanting his Boo Boo back.

BUDDY AND CHISHOLM

Cimba Johnson and her husband have a ninety-two-acre quarter-horse breeding ranch. Buddy, a big bay gelding, was the only boy on the place. His best friend was a buckskin mare named Sunset. Buddy and Sunset spent fifteen years together, until Buddy, in his old age, finally had to be put down.

In spring of the year following Buddy's death, Chisholm was born. The big bay colt was very weak, and only after a visit to an equine emergency clinic was he stabilized. A few months later he had to have surgery to correct his knock-knees. Ordinarily, Cimba and her husband sell all the foals they raise, but because of Chisholm's problems, they decided to keep him and had him gelded. Once again the mares had a big bay gelding in their midst.

Buddy

Cimba and her husband began to have inklings of Chisholm's true identity when everyone who came to see him who had also

Cimba and Chisholm

known Buddy would step back and say, "Do you realize he looks exactly like Buddy?" So many features were similar. Both horses were huge and stocky, with a wide chest and a front left leg that was not quite straight. Each had hind legs that turned inward, an elongated head, black-tipped ears, and a mule-colored nose. They were also similar in temperament: both horses could get along with any person and any horse.

When Chisholm recovered enough from knee surgery to be put out in the field, he was placed in a pasture next to Sunset's; she herself was way up on top of a ridge. When Chisholm came out, Sunset threw up her head, nickered, and ran at top speed down the hill and over to the fence. Chisholm met her there, and the two horses stayed together for hours, rubbing noses and grazing at the fence line. This behavior was extremely unusual for Sunset, who was the lead mare and typically bossy.

She normally squealed at new horses to put them in their place, but Sunset never once squealed at Chisholm.

Chisholm exhibits some peculiar behaviors that Buddy once did. Like Buddy, Chisholm loves to rest his chin and head on a person's shoulder and could stand for hours that way. He is also, like Buddy before him, the only horse on the farm who likes bananas. Cimba hand-fed Buddy all the bananas he could eat on the day they put him down.

Cimba and her husband feel that Chisholm is Buddy reincarnated and that the little colt did everything he could to make sure he stayed around long enough for them to realize that. He spent months wiggling his way into their hearts to give them the time they needed to see who he really was.

PEBBLES

Pebbles is a black-and-white harlequin Great Dane. Her person, Kathy Vryndle, got Pebbles at twelve weeks old from a breeder who had kept the puppies outside in a kennel. Kathy knew that Pebbles had never been inside a house. Nevertheless, when she arrived home and opened the door to the house for Pebbles, the gangly puppy ran through the house directly to the kitchen. Once there, she got up on one of the chairs at the table and serenely surveyed her domain.

Kathy said she knew instantly that Pebbles had to be her deceased boxer, Dino, returning. Kathy's daughter had taught Dino this same trick — to sit in a chair at the table with the family while they were eating.

Another behavior also matches Dino's. Though Pebbles will lick everyone else on the face, she refuses to lick Kathy. Even after

Pebbles

having spent months in quarantine following a move to Hawaii, Pebbles greeted Kathy in her usual manner: she bowed her head and placed her forehead on Kathy's heart, exactly as Dino always used to do. A skeptic might quip that Kathy just has bad breath, but anyone who knows dogs knows that for a dog, bad breath would be an *incentive* to lick someone, not a deterrent!

CRICKET

My friend and fellow communicator Lena Swanson told me an extraodinary story about an exchange she had with a cat at an advanced animal-communication class she once attended.[7] The class had been given a list of questions to ask one of their own animals, and Lena had decided to work with her golden retriever. She took a break before starting the exercise, and when she went downstairs to the bathroom, she encountered her teacher's cat Cricket, a short-haired calico who had been described as extremely shy and not fond of being held or handled. In fact, the students had been told they probably would not even get a glimpse of Cricket. But when Lena came out of the bathroom, Cricket was still there, and as she passed her she heard the cat say, "I want to talk to you."

Lena was surprised but told Cricket she would be back to talk after she got something to eat. When she returned to the basement she found Cricket waiting for her. Lena decided to do the class exercise with Cricket instead of with her own dog, since the cat seemed so insistent, so she started asking Cricket the questions on the list the teacher had handed out. The questions were pretty straightforward: What do you like to do? What kind of food do you like? Where do you like to sleep? Who is your best friend? Cricket answered with short, precise phrases. Then Lena asked, "Do you have any complaints?"

Instead of answering the question Cricket responded, "We've known each other in a past life. That's why I wanted to talk to you."

Lena was stunned. "What?" she asked.

Cricket replied, "Times of castles. King and queen times."

"What are you talking about?" Lena asked.

"You think about it," said Cricket.

All of a sudden, memories came flooding back to Lena. "You were a prince and I was a servant — your lover," she stammered.

"Yes, and it's nice to see you again," said Cricket.

Lena could not believe the information she was receiving, but she also could not stop herself from crying. She was actually sobbing. The memories she had of this cat/prince were strong

Lena and client

and vivid. Lena felt like she was losing her mind. It is one thing
to have a feeling that an animal has been with you previously as
a cat or a dog or a horse, as the other stories in this chapter suggest; it's quite another to contemplate a past life where you and
an animal were both humans or both animals. There is no way
to prove the information Lena received and probably no reason to
attempt to do so. If you find it unbelievable, that's understand-
able, and you may just want to skip ahead to the next story in
this chapter — otherwise, read on. At this point in the
encounter she tried to get back to normal by asking another
question on the list. "What do you dream of?" she said.

Cricket replied, "I dream of being with you in a future life.
And now I want to stop talking."

With that the cat did stop talking, so Lena reached out to pat
her and end the exercise. Cricket was extremely affectionate and
responsive to her touch, not at all like her owner had described
her. Lena said it took hours to recover from that conversation.

She felt as if she had been temporarily insane. However, a part of her felt the information must have been true, because of the intensity of the emotions and images the exchange with Cricket had evoked.

Days later, when she had recovered somewhat, Lena had further conversations with Cricket about the life they had supposedly shared in the past. As the details became clearer, she realized that the intense emotion she felt was tied to a tragic ending in that lifetime: the cat told her that her affair with the prince had been discovered, and that Lena had been executed. There are a number of compelling factors about this account, chief among them being that Lena had no intention of even talking to Cricket in the first place. She had simply walked past the cat. When she started interviewing Cricket, her only expectation was to get answers to a list of rather mundane questions. The emotions and memories that her conversation with Cricket stirred up were so totally unbidden, and so extraordinary, that Lena is convinced she could not have just made them up. Lena is also one of the more down-to-earth people I know. Before becoming an animal communicator, she taught English as a second language for fifteen years to Laotian students in the Minneapolis school system. She is grounded and levelheaded. I just can't see her inventing that story out of whole cloth. Further, her communication with Cricket conformed to two fairly reliable indicators of a genuine intuitive exchange: the information was highly unusual, and Lena had a strong feeling that it was true.

TAMARA

Tamara was an old, overweight, asthmatic mare whom Nancy Stephens credits with one of the most profound experiences of her life. Tamara belonged to a friend with whom Nancy boarded her own horses. One day, while Nancy was at her friend's farm with the blacksmith and his apprentice, all three of them were shocked when Tamara groaned and fell over dead in her stall. Moments before, she had been happily munching hay with no sign of distress.

A few seconds after her last breath, they saw a flash of glittery light rise slowly from Tamara's body. It was as if time were suspended. The flash looked like a sparkly, rainbow-colored helix. Nancy's two horses threw their heads up as the light ascended.

Nancy's blacksmith said, "What the hell was that?"

They all were shaken, and after comparing notes, they realized they all had seen the same thing. They concluded that it must have been Tamara's spirit leaving her body.

This was a life-altering event for Nancy. Over the previous few years her faith had been shaken to the core by various difficult life events, including the untimely death of family members. She also had a debilitating fear of death, and she was always overcome with sorrow at loss of life, whether human or animal. Seeing Tamara's spirit rise from the horse's body changed everything. It eased Nancy's sorrow at the loss of loved ones. It restored her faith in the process of renewal and showed her that all creatures have spirits that live on. Death ceased to be so frightening.

Nancy will be grateful to Tamara forever. She said if she could give one gift to every person on earth, it would be to experience what she did as she watched the light leave Tamara's body. She thinks animals already know all about this. Now, whenever a loved one dies, the memory of Tamara's gift comforts her like nothing else can.

JENNY

When Jenny, my parents' Norwich terrier, got very old and became too difficult for them to care for, I took her in. I had two Jennys at the time, as Jenny my cat was with me then also. Jenny the Norwich lived with me for almost two years. She couldn't see or hear, and she was completely dependent on me, but she remained a feisty terrier to the end. I finally had her put down when she was no longer interested in eating and was having trouble standing up. I took her to my veterinarian, who very gently euthanized her. I gave instructions for her to be cremated, said my good-byes, and left her body there on the table. I was surprised to find that her death upset me, because when animals have had a long, happy life I usually do not get upset by their deaths. But I was really sad for the rest of the day. Then I realized why. It was because I could no longer help Jenny. She had to make the journey into death on her own.

A few days later, I got a call from Meagan Avants, one of the technicians at the clinic. She wanted me to know what had happened when she went in to get Jenny's body. As she stood looking down at Jenny, the swinging door to the exam room cracked open just wide enough for something the size of a little Norwich terrier to walk through, and then it swung closed again. There was no wind or vibration. Nothing could have made the door open. Megan knew it was Jenny's spirit leaving the room. She told me that she often gets these kinds of messages and often plays the role of messenger for animals who have died. She said Jenny just wanted me to know that she was okay and that she was continuing on her journey without me.

Suggested Practices

SAYING GOOD-BYE

My dog Dougal, a chocolate Lab–Irish wolfhound cross, died very suddenly at the age of fifteen when a tumor on his heart burst. He was unconscious before I realized he was dying, and I never got to say good-bye. If your animal is nearing the end of life, take the opportunity to say out loud why you are happy that he or she came into your life and what you learned from the experience.

If, like me, you lost an animal before you were able to adequately say good-bye, you can still talk with the animal in spirit, as I did later with Dougal. Just close your eyes and imagine the animal in front of you. Speak out loud, say everything you wanted to say but didn't get a chance to, and assume that your animal can hear and understand every word.

ASK FOR A SIGN

Ask your current animal to give you a sign if he or she has been with you before, and pay attention to any subsequent behaviors on the part of your animal that are suggestive of an animal that was with you before.

COMING BACK

If you believe in reincarnation, tell your animals (past or present) that you would like them to come back to you in another form in this lifetime, if it's possible and if they would like to. My feeling is that if your animals decide to return to you, they will find you. You don't have to go looking for them. Just ask them to make it obvious when they return, and then be alert for signs. These could include encountering animals in unusual circumstances, feeling an immediate, profound connection to a strange animal, or actually hearing a message from an animal, as Jeanne Owen did from her horse Cisco.

CHAPTER EIGHT

SPIRITUAL JOURNEYS

I always warn my students that learning intuitive communication with animals and nature is a spiritual journey that will probably change their lives. I say this because to communicate well, you must learn to recognize and trust your own inner wisdom. That alone is a radical shift for most of us. Once you start telling people what you're doing, you will have to learn to endure being ridiculed and trivialized by some. That will make you strong. And if you continue with the practice, you will almost certainly be led on a far different path from the one on which you started.

I also tell my students that they are the pioneers, leading the way for everyone else. Some, like me, have chosen to do this work as a vocation. The stories in this chapter are about several people who became professionals in this field — where they started and what their journeys entailed.

JEANNIE

Jeannie Andre's journey started with the purchase of her first horse, when she was forty-two. She had vowed to herself that she would have a horse before she died. When her dream finally came true, she was unprepared for the reality of owning a huge animal with a will of its own. The mare she bought was frightened out of her wits, and so was Jeannie. Neither had any idea what to do. Jeanie was so afraid of her "dream horse" that she would become nauseated on the way to the barn each day. But like a moth to a flame, she was drawn by an overwhelming desire to love that horse.

She named the untrained, three-and-a-half-year-old mare Angel. It was quite a misnomer. At her boarding stable, Angel became known as the kicking, biting dragon-horse to steer clear of. The other boarders at the barn had bets on how long the relationship would last, and they frequently asked Jeannie why she had wanted the mare in the first place. After a few months Jeannie got lucky and came across the help she needed. A woman she'd met during her horse-shopping days offered to teach her the basics of natural horsemanship, training that uses positive reinforcement and other techniques based on the study of horse behavior.

Jeannie spent hours with Angel practicing the exercises, which involved making Angel yield and respond by moving her feet. The exercises had a positive effect on how Angel related to Jeannie, and to Jeannie's surprise and delight, any little success ended up being fun for Angel too. In tiny increments, Jeannie became Angel's leader. They began to trust each other, and throughout the process of building a relationship, they each stayed safe and were never bored.

Jeannie and Angel

Jeannie has weathered a lot of challenges in her life. For two years, she cared for a friend who was dying of lung cancer. When she was in her twenties, she moved from a small town to downtown Manhattan. She has gone skydiving, walked barefoot over hot coals, and sung solo with a full orchestra in front of thousands of people in Paris and at the great pyramids in Egypt. But, Jeannie said, nothing compares to the experience of developing a relationship with Angel.

After about three years, the two had perfected their skills, and they started giving public demonstrations to show others the possibilities of natural horsemanship. In these demonstrations, which they still do regularly, Jeannie works with Angel untethered and asks her verbally to change gaits, change directions, stop on a dime, back up the length of the arena, gallop toward her, and stop at her feet. As part of the demonstration, she climbs a fence and calls Angel over to line up against the fence so Jeannie can mount and ride bareback, using just a thin string around Angel's neck for guidance.

During a demonstration one day, after Angel had been running for a while, Jeannie turned to the audience to explain what she'd gone through to earn Angel's cooperation and trust. Angel decided that was a good time for a break and headed for a water bucket on the other side of the arena. Jeannie turned to Angel and said, "I'm not sure you should drink right now, so soon after you ran." Immediately, Angel stopped and backed up about fifty feet, until she was standing right next to Jeannie. It was as if she had understood every word. After that Jeannie began noticing that Angel anticipated her requests, and eventually she realized that Angel was reading her mind.

Shortly thereafter, her dying cat, Sparky, provided the impetus for Jeannie to contact an animal communicator. She had a very strong feeling that Sparky did not want her to assist him, but wanted to die on his own at home — which he did. A communicator, who had only been told that Sparky died but not how or why, confirmed that he had wanted to go on his own without any help. Inspired by that experience, Jeannie decided to study intuitive communication herself. She now does consultations for people and incorporates her intuitive abilities into the demonstrations and teaching she and Angel do.

Jeannie and Angel function as a therapy team. They both understand how fear feels, and because of that they can put beginning riders, and people who are drawn to but afraid of horses, at ease. Together, they help new riders develop horsemanship skills and open people's minds and hearts to the fact that there is "someone home" inside each animal in our world.

MICHELE

I met Michele Arnold Limacher through my workshops. An accomplished pianist, she worked in orchestra management before she began studying animal communication. She had taken one previous workshop from another communicator and loved it so much that she decided to switch her vocation to animal healing. She was taking any classes she could find related to that subject. Her husband had a well-paying job, which allowed Michele to quit working for a while.

I always call Michele my best student, and she always says I am her best teacher, but in reality, I think my cat Jenny turned out to be Michele's best teacher. At Michele's first workshop, I led the group in a journey to find an animal guide. I instructed them to sit comfortably, or lie on the floor, and imagine traveling to another location and meeting and interacting with an animal. Michele found she could not get comfortable, even lying on the floor. She felt nervous and insecure about taking this imaginary journey and had vague fears of becoming lost or confused while doing it. At that point, Jenny jumped onto Michele's stomach and curled up. Michele said she instantly felt grounded and safe and was able to go ahead with the journey.

After that, Michele began doing a lot of journeying on her own. She said Jenny often showed up (in spirit) on these journeys and helped her to feel comfortable. When I saw Michele again I could tell something had changed. She seemed more confident and animated, more relaxed and comfortable in her body.

Michele ended up taking all my workshops. Since she has no animals of her own, and she had to practice, she tried it with her plants. She made peace with her unruly dieffenbachia, and rather than finding it a new home, she learned to love the plant. She finally got her Christmas cactus to bloom, just by talking to it. She interviewed her sickly spider plant and found out that it wanted rocks covered with water placed in a tray nearby. When she installed these features, it revived and became robust. She said she now hears what her plants want as she walks by them.

Michele

Michele recalls having always been deeply connected to plants and nature. As a child she would go to the woods and just sit, feeling somehow in sync with nature. She is passionate about trees, although she can't explain why.

She now works professionally as an animal and nature communicator and often takes inner journeys to seek answers and assistance for people and animals who have unresolved problems in

Michele's Christmas cactus

their lives. She sees her work as a sort of backdoor form of med-
itation and spiritual practice — a softer, quicker, easier way for
people to connect with all that is. Every day she tunes in intuitively
to nature, insects, the sun, and the trees and advises others to do
that too, even if, like Michele, they live in the middle of a city.

GERRIE

I recall a TV show from my childhood named *Queen for a
Day*. Each program had three women contestants who talked
about the disastrous events of their lives; one's husband might
have died of cancer, while another's child had been maimed
in a car accident. After each contestant spoke, the show's host
would hold his hand over the woman's head, and the audience

would applaud. The woman who got the most applause, for having the most pitiful life, would win a prize. When I asked my former student Gerrie Huits, who now practices animal communication professionally, if intuitive communication had changed her life, her response reminded me of that program.

Gerrie and client

According to Gerrie, her journey into intuitive communication began when she had a conflict with the board of directors of the nonprofit mental-health group she worked for. The situation got so bad that she lost her job. Then her father became ill and died. Then all three of her dogs, her cat, and two of her best friends died. Then she found out that her boyfriend was a sex addict who was having relationships with other women, including a friend of hers. Her boyfriend went into therapy, was diagnosed as manic-depressive, and was admitted to a psychiatric hospital for seven months. Gerrie had to go to the hospital too, because of trouble with her digestive system. Then she had a conflict with a different board of directors, one that ran a woman's bookstore where she volunteered, and she had to stop working there too. By this time her neck, shoulders, and back hurt so badly that she could hardly move. She underwent months of physiotherapy, and then she grew depressed herself and became a virtual hermit.

Finally realizing she needed more help, Gerrie found a good therapist, who had her start doing intuitive painting, and soon after that, her life began to turn around. She broke up with her boyfriend, moved into her own place, and adopted two cats from a local shelter. She returned to studying and practicing Reiki, a form of energy healing she had done in the past. She took up running again. Little by little, she began to feel better, good things started to happen, and soon she felt well enough to go back to work.

But every time she looked at the job listings in the newspaper, she got extremely ill. Something was not right. She kept remembering a palm reading she had been given years before. The reader told her that at age forty-eight, she would start doing work that she had always wanted to do. But Gerrie could not figure out what that might be. Her brother told her it probably had to do with animals, so she started thinking about working in a zoo or at an animal shelter, or becoming a veterinarian. But she felt in her heart that those jobs would not suit her.

A few months after she turned forty-eight, her mother called to tell her to watch an animal program on TV that was featuring a communicator. She thought it might cheer Gerrie up.

When Gerrie saw the program, she immediately knew that this was what she had been waiting for.

She began studying intuitive communication, and from that day on, her life changed rapidly and completely for the good. She found her heartfelt passion and ultimate goal in life: communication with and assisting animals and nature as much as she could. She now feels that all the bad things that happened to her were necessary to get her attention, wake her up, and clear the way for her true calling.

Until she started this work, Gerrie had felt isolated and disconnected from the world, even though she had always had good friends and a supportive family and had been professionally successful. Entering the world of intuitive communication brought a deep connection with the world around her, a feeling she had never had before, and one that made her very happy. She is beginning to understand the idea that there is a "greater plan" for everything, and to feel there is a love that unites all life. This understanding humbles her and motivates her to live life to the fullest, working hard but also enjoying it as much as she can. One of her cats won't let her forget this. "I am here," she told Gerrie, "to remind you to enjoy life in spite of all the suffering."

Suggested Practice

Ask to be guided on your true path in life. Then follow your heart and pay attention to your intuition.

CHAPTER NINE	A BETTER WORLD IS POSSIBLE

I would imagine that most of you reading this book care very deeply about animals and nature and are as upset as I am about the state of our earth and the crises we face. Because I have to address suffering every day in my work, in the form of unhappy, lost, ill, or dying animals, I've had to learn how to deal with intense negative emotions while simultaneously working to effect positive change. This is part of the process of opening up to communication with nonhumans.

Often my students and clients ask for help in learning how to cope with the grief that can accompany a deepening intuitive awareness of the world. In this final chapter I share with you what I have learned about how to stay aware of the crises we face, process the intense feelings that surface, and still take effective action for change. I offer this support as one lover of the planet to another, facing as we do an unprecedented threat to the continuation of life. I believe there is a chance to turn things around, and that a better world is possible.

OUR TIMES

Dickens would probably concede that our present age is really the best and the worst of times. Worst, because life on earth is more in peril than at any other time in recorded history. (The scientists who contest that statement tend to be the ones paid by governments and corporations to obscure the truth.) Best, because of the compassion and innovation that is everywhere evident.

You won't hear the good news from the mainstream media, though. For that you have to go to alternative sources such as *Positive News, Yes!* magazine, and *Ode* magazine, which feature stories of hope, innovation, and resourcefulness from around the globe.[1] Those journals recount efforts to undo the damage and create a compassionate, sustainable world. Here are some examples:

- A women-led, democratic, grassroots water-conservation movement, expanding rapidly throughout India, is counteracting a drought caused by the Green Revolution, a worldwide corporate-sponsored water-intensive agriculture program.[2]

- Australian scientists have discovered an inexpensive way to produce clean hydrogen power and are only a few years away from being able to implement a large-scale production plant.[3]

- A man in London installed solar panels on his house and built a curbside electric charger for his car. He now powers his car with fuel he has collected directly from the sun.[4]

- An engineer in Vermont has designed an organic wastewater treatment system that uses microbes, plants, and animals to turn wastewater into potable water. The system can be used to restore bodies of water damaged by pollution.[5]

- Activists from Europe, Canada, and the United States are collaborating to promote the humane treatment of livestock.[6]

- Inexpensive solar cookers are being used to offset the use of wood and consequent deforestation in third-world countries.[7]

- The city government of Burlington, Vermont, is working to make the city sustainable through energy conservation, composting and community supported agriculture, and energy cogeneration projects. The energy conservation program alone has saved the community 4.3 million dollars so far.[8]

- Environmental protection has been afforded to 1.3 billion acres of Canada's subarctic forests by the Canadian government.[9]

- The 2004 World Social Forum brought together eighty thousand social-change activists from 132 countries in a conference to collaborate for positive change internationally.[10]

- A researcher has discovered that fungi can be used to clean up toxic waste sites and restore degraded habitats.[11]

It's clear that we have the ingenuity to live in a way that sustains life, using solar and alternative fuels, growing food at the local level, and using water conservation and innovative restoration techniques for water treatment and waste remediation. This dream is possible, and it is not too late.

Standing in the way, according to analyses by groups such as CorpWatch, are the larger governments and top corporations of our world, which are more concerned with political and financial domination than with the survival of the planet or the welfare of its people.[12] But even on that issue you can find a bright spot if you go looking. For example, I found an article about how some U.S. cities are acting independently to curb greenhouse gas emissions, even as the administration of George W. Bush works to undermine international efforts to stop global warming.[13] In another article, an economic analyst suggests that the simple solution to corporate despotism is to make a company's shareholders liable for the corporation's misdeeds.[14]

Good news, though, does not by itself affect the magnitude of our plight.

FEELING THE WORLD

It can be hard to cope with how bad things are. It's tempting just to shut down, stop listening, and shut out the bad news. However, the problems won't resolve themselves. Humans made these problems, and only we can undo them. I believe that animals and other beings of nature are acutely aware of the global danger now upon us and are urging us to stay connected and take action. They are also asking us not to abandon them or turn off our awareness of their dire situation.

According to Australian physician Helen Caldicott, co-founder of the group Physicians for Social Responsibility, even if you were able to suppress negative feelings, they'd manifest themselves in other ways, as chronic depression, illness, addiction to drugs, or addictive consumerism.[15] You have to work through your grief about the state of the world to be able to be of any assistance. Caldicott's remedy? Find one helpful thing to do and start doing it. That is the best tactic I've found, too. Choose what you want to do to help, and then devote yourself to it. Tell yourself that you can do only what you can do, and have faith that your action is making a difference.

GET BUSY

In the suggested practices at the end of this chapter I offer some ideas about how to choose which issue you want to pursue from among the many options available. The action you decide to take could be as simple as joining an organization and helping with its efforts. Or you could come up with a creative new solution to a problem. Every successful effort for positive change started out as an idea in the mind of just one person.

Once you get involved, you may eventually find yourself in the typical activist's bind of doing too much and getting so invested that you burn out. If you are an activist now, you may already be in that spot. The solution to that problem is to work smart.

WORK SMART

Walter Greist is one of the scientists I contacted during my research for this book. He is now an organic farmer and no longer working in the field of intuition and psychic (or psi) research, but he still retains a keen interest. He sent me an unpublished graduate paper about one of his psi experiments, in which he worked with two groups of people. He left the first group in a room, where the participants listened to an audiotape he had made that recounted a true adventure he'd experienced. The narrative stopped before the story ended, and the people in the group were given five possible endings to the story and told to guess the real ending from among them.

The second group also listened to the tape, but Greist was in the room with them. When that group had to guess the end of the story, Greist was right there, mentally sending them information about the actual ending. The people in the second group still had to guess, but they had the benefit of Greist's directed thoughts in making that guess. He repeated the experiment with a number of stories. The results showed that the people in the second group, who heard the anecdotes and were additionally exposed to the researcher's mental communications, were significantly more accurate in choosing the correct ending than the first group, which had the benefit only of Greist's recorded voice.[16] Thus, Greist found that the process of guessing was enhanced when, unbeknownst to the participants, he added a psi component to augment it.

According to physicists such as Russell Targ, the physics of making change in the world appears to have a similar dynamic.[17] To be most effective, you need to take action in the real world but bolster it with some *unseen* metaphysical or spiritual component. This could be the simple act of praying, or you could try out one of the techniques for bringing your dreams to life that I describe in the exercises at the end of this chapter.

Including a spiritual component with your action counteracts burnout and makes your real-world action stronger. It helps you to work "smart." It's like having an internal power source (your prayer or other internal work) and an external power source (the visible action you take in the world). Each one enhances the other.

CREATING THE CHANGE YOU WANT TO SEE IN THE WORLD

A vast number of books exist on positive thinking, visualization, and other mental techniques that people have found helpful for creating a positive change in some area of their lives, or in the world. Such techniques, popularly referred to as methods for manifesting change, can be used to improve a bad situation or to attract the things and people you want into your life. Wayne Dyer is a well-known proponent of manifesting. In his book *The Power of Intention*, Dyer goes into detail about physics theories that support the idea that we can actually change reality simply through our thoughts and emotional intentions.[18] Suzanna Stinnett, a student of mine, is also an author. She has written about the process of shifting reality through thought patterns.[19] She learned an important lesson about this from a communication she had with a young whale. The whale had been in the news because he was coming too close to shore. Suzanna's first message to the baby whale, as she stood on the bluff watching it, was to send the thought that she was worried. Immediately she got back a response from the whale saying that this is exactly what humans are doing wrong: we worry and imagine the worst in any given situation, and as a consequence, we attract that to ourselves.

The next day Suzanna was in a café and overheard a couple discussing the whale. They were looking at a photo in the paper taken the day before and saying things like, "The children in that picture are too close to the whale. I wonder if they were throwing rocks at it." Suzanna had been there when the photo was taken and knew that the children had been completely respectful and, indeed, in awe of the whale. The truth of what the whale had told her hit home. She realized that the whale was right: negative thoughts can take on an energy and a life of their own, and humans engage in negative thoughts to an excessive and destructive degree.

To change this bad habit, here is a summary of the techniques I have learned so far in my life about how to use your thoughts, feelings, and visualizations to change reality.

- First, identify what it is you want to bring into reality. It can be anything you dream about having — an object, experience, or outcome — for yourself or for the world.

- Be 100 percent committed to your dream, and take actions in the real world that completely support its realization. Act, in everything you do, as if you have already achieved it.

- Create the emotional feelings you would have if your dream were already reality. These positive feelings are the fuel that propels a dream to life.

- Most important, if you find yourself falling into negative thinking, stop immediately. Give yourself the mental instruction, "Cancel that thought!" Then replace the negative thought with a series of counterbalancing positive ones. The idea is to eventually train yourself not to think negatively, because, if the physicists are correct, you are what you think.

- Finally, as you go about your day imagining your dream already fulfilled, say a silent thank-you to the universe.

When you start using these techniques, you will find that some things materialize very quickly. Others may take more time. Making your dreams come true could turn out to be the hardest thing you attempt in your life. The key to success is to keep at it and always believe that your dream is possible.

Suggested Practices

Following are further suggested techniques for bringing your dreams for the world to life. As mentioned, you can adapt these same techniques for your personal dreams and goals as well.

CHOOSING YOUR FOCUS

It is best to choose an issue to focus on that you are passionate about; then you can decide on what action you want to pursue. Make a list of the top ten things you would most like to see change in the world, and pick the one thing on the list that you feel most strongly about.

CHOOSING AN ACTION

There are two ways to approach this — logically and intuitively. To take the logical approach, search the Internet or at the library to find out who may be working on the issue you have selected. You probably will find many organizations already committed to addressing it. Make a list of the organizations that most appeal to you and research each one until you find the one that is the best match for you. Contact the organization to see if there is a way for you to help that seems productive to you. Alternatively, you could brainstorm creative ways to address the issue you have selected and follow up with some independent, innovative action.

The intuitive approach would be to ask for guidance on what your most effective action should be. If you like, go sit in a favorite place in nature and ask the universe for this guidance. Then pay attention to any signs or symbols that appear as signposts along the path to action.

BRINGING YOUR VISION TO LIFE

In their latest book on how to manifest your desires, Jerry and Esther Hicks advise us to be continually vigilant about what we intend before we actually engage in an action.[20] If you have the expectation of a positive outcome, it becomes self-fulfilling. Even if something seems hopeless, intend that the outcome be positive. These authors also advise that you constantly imagine scenes of your dream coming true. Create short scenarios of this in your mind and repeat them over and over whenever you have a free moment. By doing this, you are laying a mental track, as it were, down which a positive event can travel to come into being.

Wayne Dyer advises you to think from the end. How would you be acting and thinking if what you wanted were already accomplished? Act that way and think that way now. One of

Dyer's techniques involves closing your eyes and seeking out what you feel to be the deepest level of your being. From that vantage point, believe that what you want is possible and that you are capable of achieving it.

A final suggestion is to consult your own intuition to find help on how to best achieve your desires. You can ask that guidance come to you in your dreams as you sleep. Or you can ask for direction through a regular practice of automatic writing. For a start, try writing continuously for fifteen minutes without stopping to think or choose words. When you read what you have written you will likely find that the process of spontaneous writing has allowed your intuition to come through and provide you with the guidance you needed.

WHAT THE FUTURE HOLDS

The universe begins to look more like a great thought than a great machine.

— SIR JAMES JEANS

This quote by astronomer Sir James Jeans expresses the essence of the future for me. It seems reasonable that the collective consciousness of the more than six billion people now alive could have a potential for positively affecting the life of this planet. Research has shown that praying for someone who is ill has a positive result.[21] Now, people around the world are experimenting with how thoughts and intentions, engaged in by masses of people, can affect larger realities.

The impact of consciousness has a central role in the Hopi prophecies about our age, which tell of coming upheavals on the earth and indicate that if humans follow the way of consciousness — the Hopi way — these changes will be lessened.[22] Most people would agree that we are heading for major change. I believe we will have to make a radical shift toward sustainable living systems if we hope to endure on the earth. If the prophecies and the physicists are correct, we can do a lot to direct the course of this time of change through the vehicle of our own thoughts and intentions.

In terms of our thoughts, we are more connected with one another than ever before thanks to the Internet. In his book *The Global Brain Awakens*, Peter Russell states that the total population of the world and our interconnected telecommunications web now resemble almost exactly the structure and patterns found in a human brain. He proposes that we are preparing to act — as a world — with one consciousness.[23]

Certainly we will be stronger collectively than each of us is in isolation. And we will be stronger still if we focus on the positive rather than giving in to fear and negativity. To any desperate or depressing situation, we should ask ourselves the "I wonder questions": I wonder what good could happen here? I wonder how this could have a good outcome? Doing so will open the door to positive change in even the worst of situations.

Unexpected help awaits us in the form of the animals and the natural world, which were once the allies of human beings. They have much to teach us, and power to help us in this time of our need. When we restore the ability to converse with them, we will revive ancient wisdom and rebuild the circle of life.

Our times require each of us to think *and* act locally *and* globally. I've volunteered thousands of hours over the past decade to create sustainable living practices in my hometown,

stop pollution, stop war, and promote a just world. I've dedicated my life to bringing the idea and skill of intuitive communication with animals and nature to as many people as possible
in the hope that this will create a favorable change in human
consciousness. Epic times call for epic actions, and we must all
get involved. A positive future for the earth lies in our hands,
like a bird, waiting to be thrown aloft and set free. The people
who love this earth far outnumber those who seek to destroy it.
What is needed now is for each of us to reconnect with our intuition and act upon what is in our hearts.

NOTES

INTRODUCTION

1 Vonda McIntyre, *Dreamsnake* (Boston: Houghton Mifflin, 1978).
2 J. Allen Boone, *Kinship with All Life* (New York: Harper and Brothers, 1954).
3 Theodore Rozak's book on this subject is *The Voice of the Earth: An Exploration of Ecopsychology* (Grand Rapids, MI: Phanes Press, 2001).
4 Vine Deloria Jr., *God Is Red: A Native View of Religion* (Golden, CO: Fulcrum Publishing, 1994), p. 292 (quote).

CHAPTER ONE

1 Margot Lasher, *And the Animals Will Teach You: Discovering Ourselves through Our Relationships with Animals* (New York: Berkeley Books, 1996).

2 T.C. McLuhan, ed., *Touch the Earth: A Self-Portrait of Indian Existence* (New York: Simon and Schuster, 1971), p. 15.

3 Karyn Sanders operates the Blue Otter Herb School in Northern California (www.karynsanders.com) and hosts *The Herbal Highway*, a radio show on Pacifica Radio (www.kfpf.org). See also Marta Williams, "Plants: The First People," *Healing Garden, The Journal for Holistic Living*, May/June 2004, p. 8.

4 Malcolm Margolin, ed., *News from Native California*, Special Reports no. 1, *California Indians and the Environment* (Berkeley, CA: Heyday Books, 1992), p. 29.

5 Peter Tompkins and Christopher Bird, *The Secret Life of Plants* (New York: HarperCollins, 1973), pp. 127–34.

6 Connie Grauds, *Jungle Medicine* (San Rafael, CA: Center for Spirited Medicine, 2004).

7 Tompkins and Bird, *The Secret Life of Plants*, pp. 17–31.

8 Sheila Ostrander and Lynn Schroeder, *The ESP Papers: Scientists Speak Out from behind the Iron Curtain* (New York: Bantam Books, 1996), pp. 41–49.

9 Marija Gimbutas, *The Civilization of the Goddess* (San Francisco: HarperSanFrancisco, 1991). For an excellent book on prehistoric artifacts and culture in Europe, see Buffie Johnson, *Lady of the Beasts: The Goddess and Her Sacred Animals* (Rochester, VT: Inner Traditions International, 1994).

10 See Lowell John Bean, ed., *California Indian Shamanism* (Menlo Park, CA: Ballena Press, 1992), p. 17, and Calvin Martin, *Keepers of the Game: Indian-Animal Relationships and the Fur Trade* (Berkeley and Los Angeles: University of California Press, 1978), pp. 33–34, 71–74.

11 Vine Deloria Jr., *God Is Red: A Native View of Religion* (Golden, CO: Fulcrum Publishing, 1994), p. 81.

12 Martin, *Keepers of the Game*, p. 17.

13 Bean, *California Indian Shamanism*, p. 16.

14 Ronald Rose, *Primitive Psychic Power* (Toronto: Signet Mystic Books, 1968).

15 Adrian Boshier, "African Apprenticeship," in *Handbook of Parapsychology and Anthropology: Proceedings of an International Conference Held in London, England, August 29–31, 1973* (New York: Parapsychology Foundation, Inc., 1974), pp. 273–87.

16 Russell Targ, *Limitless Mind: A Guide to Remote Viewing and Transformation of Consciousness* (Novato, CA: New World Library, 2004), pp. 5–6.

17 Russell Targ, *Miracles of the Mind: Exploring Nonlocal Consciousness and Spiritual Healing* (Novato, CA: New World Library, 1999), pp. 45–51.

18 Targ, *Limitless Mind*, p. 7.

19 Ibid., pp. 7–13.

20 David Bohm, *The Undivided Universe* (New York: Routledge, 1995).

21 Rupert Sheldrake, *Dogs That Know When Their Owners Are Coming Home and Other Unexplained Powers of Animals* (New York: Crown Publishers, 1999).

22 A friend of Moonhawk's has posted his work at www.enformy.com. You might want to download it if you find it interesting; it is sure to be in rare supply unless someone decides to publish it.

23 Danny K. Alford, "The Origin of Speech in a Deep Structure of Psi," *New Directions in the Study of Man* 2, no. 2 (Fall/Winter 1978). Available at www.enformy.com.

24 Danny K. Alford, *Not Just Words, Redux: The Newsletter of Language and Consciousness* 1, no. 1 (March 2002): p. 8. Available at www.enformy.com.

25 Email to David Peat from Dan Moonhawk Alford, March 12, 2000. Available at www.enformy.com.

CHAPTER THREE

1 Ronald Rose, *Primitive Psychic Power* (Toronto: Signet Mystic Books, 1968).

2 Rupert Sheldrake, *Dogs That Know When Their Owners Are Coming Home and Other Unexplained Powers of Animals* (New York: Crown Publishers, 1999).

3 To see Star's photographs of marine mammals, visit her website at www.stardewar.com.

CHAPTER FOUR

1 Margot Lasher, *And the Animals Will Teach You: Discovering Ourselves through Our Relationships with Animals* (New York: Berkeley Books, 1996), pp. 38–39.

2 Natural horsemanship techniques utilize horse behavior patterns to direct a horse to work as a team with a human being. The goal is to achieve good behavior through positive, nonviolent methods. TTEAM is a specific form of nonviolent ground training developed by Linda Tellington Jones. TTouch is her unique bodywork system for animals. To learn more, visit http://ttouch.com. Parelli Natural Horsemanship is another method of training horses using nonviolent methods. To learn about it, visit http://www.parelli.com. Carolyn Resnick has developed a system of training based on her years spent with mustangs

in the wild. Her book on this subject is *Naked Liberty* (Los Olivos, CA: Amigo Publications, 2005).

3 The natural trim, or barefoot trim, approximates what a wild horse hoof is like. This method encourages people to keep their horses barefoot. To learn about the natural trim, see the websites listed in the Web Resources section.

4 Dianne Skafte, *When Oracles Speak: Understanding the Signs and Symbols All Around Us* (Wheaton, IL: Quest Books, 2000).

5 Belleruth Naparstek, *Your Sixth Sense: Activating Your Psychic Potential* (New York: HarperCollins, 1997).

CHAPTER FIVE

1 To view Lori's work, visit her website at www.dandelionpress.com.

2 To have pursued that course of action legally in the United States, one would have to obtain permission from governmental authorities.

CHAPTER SEVEN

1 After many years of doing this work, I now believe that all life forms possess a spirit that transcends the physical. In my research, I discovered that this type of belief is found in most indigenous cultures past and present. In indigenous cosmology, humans, animals, trees, and all aspects of nature are represented in the spirit world, as expressed in the following quote from a Paiute medicine man: "We do believe in life after death. The many deities and spirits come from that belief. We return in the form of animals, trees, birds, spirits, and other forms. We are part of the whole.

We are the whole. We are part of the spirit world now. We will be part of it in the future. We have always been part of it. All things are one, and all life is one in one circle of time." Antonia Mills and Richard Slobodin, *Amerindian Rebirth: Reincarnation Belief among North American Indians and Inuit* (Toronto: University of Toronto Press, 1994), 1.

In marked contrast to indigenous belief systems, many modern religions consider humans to have exclusive or preferential entitlement to spirituality, while animals and other aspects of nature are either devoid of spirit or considered spiritually inferior to humans. To me, this is another expression of the separation and alienation of humans from the rest of nature, common in modern culture and absent in aboriginal culture.

2   Rescue remedy is a mixture of flower essences helpful for calming the emotions. It is made by setting flowers in water and then removing them. The water is said to take on the vibration of the flower. The formula is liquid and is taken internally or rubbed on the skin.

3   Ignacia amara is a homeopathic remedy available in pill form and it is taken internally.

4   To find a holistic veterinarian in the United States, visit www.ahvma.org.

5   My experience of this is that when an animal you love dies, the animal's spirit stays close to you until you are strong enough to go on alone. Then whenever you think of that animal or invoke it in any way, the spirit is right back with you. I tell people that they never completely lose the animals they love, and that they are never truly alone. Many of my clients report experiences of their animals showing them they are still near in spirit. One client told me she found

her dog's muddy footprints on the rug and then watched in amazement as the footprints slowly faded away. Another repeatedly tripped over her cat's long-lost toys, which kept appearing mysteriously in the middle of the kitchen floor. She said she knew it was her cat's spirit greeting her.

6 As far as I am aware, there has been no scholarly examination of reincarnation in animals. There are many such works regarding evidence of reincarnation in humans. However, this concept is not widely accepted in Western culture. Eastern religions that incorporate a belief in reincarnation still typically perpetuate a separation between humans and other life, ascribing a spiritually superior status to human beings. Mills and Slobidin found that American Indian and Inuit cultures have complex belief structures about reincarnation, and that most often they emphasize the spiritual equality of all forms of life. See *Amerindian Rebirth*.

7 Lena is an animal communicator who incorporates spiritual journeying and does a lot of work on a spiritual level with animals. To learn more about this you can visit her website at www.lenaswanson.com.

CHAPTER NINE

1 For *Positive News*, see http://positivenews.org.uk. For *Yes!* magazine, see www.yesmagazine.org. For *Ode* magazine, see www.odemagazine.com.

2 Vandana Shiva, "Turning Scarcity into Abundance," *Yes!*, Winter 2004.

3 "Unlimited New Energy from Sun and Water," *Positive News* no. 41, Autumn 2004.

4 Ibid.

5 Debra Jones, "Garbage In, Not Garbage Out," *Wired News*, January 3, 2003, http://wired.com. The website of the engineer who designed this system is www.oceanarks.org.

6 Holly Dressel, "A Better Life for Hogs," *Yes!*, Spring 2004.

7 "Solar Cooks," see *Ode* magazine's website, www.odemagazine.com/news.php?nID=198&a=true (accessed June 2005); see also www.solarcooking.org.

8 Jill Barnburg, "Pieces of the Puzzle," *Yes!*, Fall 2002.

9 Rik Langer, "Forests Win Protection," *Yes!*, Spring 2004.

10 Frances Korton, "A Report from the World Social Forum," *Yes!*, Spring 2004.

11 Linda Baker, "How Mushrooms Will Save the World," *Salon*, November 25, 2002, www.salon.com.

12 The website for CorpWatch is http://corpwatch.org./index.php.

13 "San Francisco Commits to Climate Protection Plan," *Environmental News Service*, September 28, 2004.

14 "Take Away Corporations' Privilege to Offer Shareholders Limited Financial Liability," *Ode*, Issue 20, January 2005.

15 Helen Caldicott now runs the Nuclear Policy Research Institute, a liberal think tank in Washington, D.C., whose goal is to counter the conservative think tanks that seem to have a stranglehold on American thought. See www.nuclearpolicy.org.

16 Walter Greist, "Psispeech Communication" (unpublished paper, May 22, 1976).

17 Russell Targ, *Limitless Mind: A Guide to Remote Viewing and Transformation of Consciousness* (Novato, CA: New World Library, 2004).

18 Wayne Dyer, *The Power of Intention: Learning to Co-Create Your World Your Way* (Carlsbad, NM: Hay House, 2004).

19 Suzanna Stinnett, *Little Shifts.* (Naperville, IL: Sourcebooks, Inc. 2004).

20 Jerry Hicks and Esther Hicks, *Ask and It Is Given: Learning to Manifest Your Desires* (Carlsbad, NM: Hay House, 2004).

21 Larry Dossey, *Reinventing Medicine: Beyond Mind-Body to a New Era of Healing* (San Francisco: HarperSanFrancisco, 1999).

22 Frank Walters, *Book of the Hopi* (New York: Viking Press, 1963).

23 Peter Russell, *The Global Brain Awakens: Our Next Evolutionary Leap* (Palo Alto, CA: Global Brain Inc., 1995).

BIBLIOGRAPHY

Alford, Danny K. *Not Just Words, Redux: The Newsletter of Language and Consciousness* 1, no. 1 (March 2002): 8. Available through www.enformy.com.

———. "The Origin of Speech in a Deep Structure of Psi." *New Directions in the Study of Man* 2, no. 2 (Fall/Winter 1978). Available through www.enformy.com.

Bean, Lowell John, ed. *California Indian Shamanism.* Menlo Park, CA: Ballena Press, 1992.

Bohm, David. *The Undivided Universe.* New York: Routledge, 1995.

Boone, J. Allen. *Kinship with All Life.* New York: Harper and Brothers, 1954.

Boshier, Adrian. "African Apprenticeship." In *Handbook of Parapsychology and Anthropology: Proceedings of an International Conference Held in London, England, August 29–31, 1973.* New York: Parapsychology Foundation, Inc., 1974.

Deloria, Vine Jr. *God Is Red: A Native View of Religion.* Golden, CO: Fulcrum Publishing, 1994.

Dossey, Larry. *Healing Words: The Power of Prayer and the Practice of Medicine.* New York: Harper Mass Market Paperbacks, 1997.

————. *Prayer Is Good Medicine: How to Reap the Healing Benefits of Prayer.* New York: HarperCollins, 1997.

————. *Reinventing Medicine: Beyond Mind-Body to a New Era of Healing.* San Francisco: HarperSanFrancisco, 1999.

Dyer, Wayne. *The Power of Intention: Learning to Co-Create Your World Your Way.* Carlsbad, CA: Hay House, 2004.

Gimbutas, Marija. *The Civilization of the Goddess.* San Francisco: HarperSanFrancisco, 1991.

Grauds, Connie. *Jungle Medicine.* San Rafael, CA: Center for Spirited Medicine, 2004.

Greist, Walter. "Psispeech Communication." Unpublished paper, May 22, 1976.

Hicks, Jerry. *Ask and It Is Given: Learning to Manifest Your Desires.* Carlsbad, CA: Hay House, 2004.

Johnson, Buffie. *Lady of the Beasts: The Goddess and Her Sacred Animals.* Rochester, VT: Inner Traditions International, 1994.

Lasher, Margot. *And the Animals Will Teach You: Discovering Ourselves through Our Relationships with Animals.* New York: Berkeley Books, 1996.

Macy, Joanna. *World as Lover, World as Self.* Berkeley, CA: Parallax Press, 1991.

Margolin, Malcolm, ed. *News from Native California.* Special Reports no. 1, *California Indians and the Environment.* Berkeley, CA: Heyday Books, 1992.

Martin, Calvin. *Keepers of the Game: Indian-Animal Relationships and the Fur Trade.* Berkeley and Los Angeles: University of California Press, 1978.

McIntyre, Vonda. *Dreamsnake.* Boston: Houghton Mifflin, 1978.

McLuhan, T.C., ed. *Touch the Earth: A Self-Portrait of Indian Existence.* New York: Simon and Schuster, 1971.

Mills, Antonia, and Richard Slobodin. *Amerindian Rebirth: Reincarnation Belief among North American Indians and Inuit.* Toronto: University of Toronto Press, 1994.

Naparstek, Belleruth. *Your Sixth Sense: Activating Your Psychic Potential.* New York: HarperCollins, 1997.

Ostrander, Sheila, and Lynn Schroeder. *The ESP Papers: Scientists Speak Out from behind the Iron Curtain.* New York: Bantam Books, 1996.

———. *Psychic Discoveries behind the Iron Curtain.* Englewood Cliffs, NJ: Prentice Hall Inc., 1970.

Puthoff, Charles, and Russell Targ. *The Mind Race: Understanding and Using Psychic Ability.* New York: Random House, 1984.

Radkin, Dean. *The Conscious Universe: The Scientific Truth of Psychic Phenomena.* New York: HarperCollins, 1997.

Resnick, Carolyn. *Naked Liberty.* Los Olivos, CA: Amigo Publications, 2005.

Rose, Ronald. *Primitive Psychic Power.* Toronto: Signet Mystic Books, 1968.

Rozak, Theodore. *The Voice of the Earth: An Exploration of Ecopsychology.* Grand Rapids, MI: Phanes Press, 2001.

Russell, Peter. *The Global Brain Awakens: Our Next Evolutionary Leap.* Palo Alto, CA: Global Brain, Inc., 1995.

Schwartz, Gary. *The Afterlife Experiments: Breakthrough Scientific Evidence of Life after Death.* New York: Pocket Books, 2002.

———. *The Living Energy Universe.* Charlottesville, VA: Hampton Roads Publishing Company, 1999.

Seed, John, and Joanna Macy. *Thinking Like a Mountain:*

Toward a Council of All Beings. Gabriola Island, Canada: New Society Publishers, 1988.

Sheldrake, Rupert. *Dogs That Know When Their Owners Are Coming Home and Other Unexplained Powers of Animals.* New York: Crown Publishers, 1999.

Sjoo, Monica. *Return of the Dark/Light Mother or New Age Armageddon?* Austin, TX: Plain View Press, 1999.

Skafte, Dianne. *When Oracles Speak: Understanding the Signs and Symbols All Around Us.* Wheaton, IL: Quest Books, 2000.

Stinnett, Suzanna. *Little Shifts.* Naperville, IL: Sourcebooks, Inc., 2004.

Targ, Russell. *Limitless Mind: A Guide to Remote Viewing and Transformation of Consciousness.* Novato, CA: New World Library, 2004.

Targ, Russell, and Jane Katra. *Miracles of the Mind: Exploring Nonlocal Consciousness and Spiritual Healing.* Novato, CA: New World Library, 1999.

Tompkins, Peter, and Christopher Bird. *The Secret Life of Plants.* New York: HarperCollins, 1973.

Townsend, Irving. *Separate Lifetimes.* Exeter, NH: J. N. Townsend Publishing, 1986.

Walters, Frank. *Book of the Hopi.* New York: Viking Press, 1963.

Williams, Marta. "Plants: The First People." *Healing Garden, The Journal for Holistic Living,* May/June 2004.

RECOMMENDED READING

Here are a few more books I recommend you read in addition to the books in the bibliography.

Andersen, Allen, and Linda Anderson. *Rainbows & Bridges: An Animal Companion Memorial Kit.* Novato, CA: New World Library, 2005.

Billinghurst, Ian. *Give Your Dog a Bone.* Lithgow, Australia: Self-published, 1993.

Chernak McElroy, Susan. *Animals as Teachers and Healers: True Stories and Reflections.* New York: Ballantine, 1996.

Goldstein, Martin. *The Nature of Animal Healing: The Path to Your Pet's Health, Happiness, and Longevity.* New York: Knopf, 1999.

Gurney, Carol. *The Language of Animals: 7 Steps to Communicating with Animals.* New York: Dell Trade Paperback, 2001.

Hiby, Lydia, and Bonnie Weintraub. *Conversations with Animals.* Troutdale, OR: NewSage Press, 1998.

Hill, Julia Butterfly. *The Legacy of Luna: The Story of a Tree, a Woman, and the Struggle to Save the Redwoods.* San Francisco: HarperSanFrancisco, 2001.

Hogan, Linda, and Brenda Peterson. *The Sweet Breathing of Plants: Women Writing on the Green World.* New York: North Point Press, 2001.

Ingerman, Sandra. *Soul Retrieval: Mending the Fragmented Self through Shamanic Practice.* San Francisco: HarperSanFrancisco, 1991.

Jensen, Derrick. *A Language Older Than Words.* New York: Context Books, 2000.

Kinkade, Amelia. *Straight from the Horse's Mouth: How to Talk to Animals and Get Answers.* Novato, CA: New World Library, 2005.

Kohanov, Linda. *Riding Between the Worlds: Expanding Our Potential through the Way of the Horse.* Novato, CA: New World Library, 2004.

Lauck, Joanne Elizabeth. *The Voice of the Infinite in the Small: Revisioning the Insect-Human Connection.* Mill Spring, NC: Granite Publications, 1998.

Macy, Joanna. *World As Lover, World As Self.* Berkeley, CA: Parallax Press, 1991.

Marler, Joan, ed. *From the Realm of the Ancestors.* Manchester, CT: Knowledge, Ideas, and Trends, 1997.

Masson, Jeffrey, and Susan McCarthy. *When Elephants Weep: The Emotional Lives of Animals.* New York: Bantam Doubleday Dell, 1995.

Pryor, Karen. *Don't Shoot the Dog.* New York: Bantam Books, 1984.

Rashid, Mark. *Life Lessons from a Ranch Horse*. Boulder, CO: Johnson Books, 2003.

Schultz, Mona Lisa. *Awakening Intuition: Using Your Mind-Body Network for Insight and Healing*. New York: Harmony Books, 1998.

Starhawk. *The Earth Path: Grounding Your Spirit in the Rhythms of Nature*. San Francisco: HarperSanFrancisco. 2004.

WEB RESOURCES

ALTERNATIVE/HOLISTIC VETERINARIANS

To find a holistic veterinarian in your state, visit American Holistic Veterinary Medical Association at www.ahvma.org.

ANIMAL COMMUNICATORS

The following two websites contain listings of animal communicators:

www.animaltalk.net
http://dmoz.org/Society/Paranormal/Psychic/Animals/

CAT FENCING

For a nonelectric method for keeping your cats in your backyard and keeping other cats out, visit www.catfencein.com.

COPING WITH THE DEATH OF YOUR ANIMAL

Delta Society, see pet loss and bereavement section —
http://www.deltasociety.org

Author Moira Anderson Allen's site for pet loss —
http://www.pet-loss.net

Website for Teresa Wagner, an animal communicator specializing in grief support — www.animalsinourhearts.com

JOURNALS

For information on natural methods of horse training and care, consult the *Natural Horse Journal,* www.naturalhorse.com.

LOST ANIMALS

For information on how to search for a lost animal, go to www.petrescue.com.

Sherlock Bones is a pet detective who can counsel you in how to search for your animal. Visit www.sherlockbones.com, or call 800-942-6637.

Pet Finders, a service that will phone to alert people within your area to report any sightings of your lost animal, can be contacted at www.petfindersalert.com, or by calling 800-274-2556.

NATURAL TRIM FOR HORSES

http://unitedhorsemanship.org
http://hopeforsoundness.com
http://thehorseshoof.com

NONVIOLENT TRAINING METHODS

Dogs and Cats

Karen Pryor's clicker training, a positive training method using a click noise coupled with a food or other reward: www.clickertraining.com

Also see the resources listed at www.dogwise.com.

Horses

Alexandra Kurland's clicker training, a positive training method using a click noise coupled with a food or other reward: www.theclickercenter.com

Parelli Natural Horsemanship: http://www.parelli.com

Linda Tellington Jones: http://ttouch.com

Mark Rashid: www.markrashid.com

NUTRITIONAL SUPPLEMENT COMPANIES

Dogs and Cats

www.onlynaturalpet.com

www.drgoodpet.com

www.animalessentials.com

http://dynamiteonline.com

http://herbal-treatments.com

www.helpingpetsnaturally.com

Horses

http://dynamiteonline.com

www.dropinthebucket.com

www.hiltonherbs.com

http://herbal-treatments.com

INDEX

ABOUT THE AUTHOR

*M*arta Williams got her undergraduate degree in natural resource conservation at the University of California at Berkeley and her master's degree in biology at San Francisco State University. Before becoming an animal communicator, she worked for many years as a wildlife biologist and environmental scientist.

The author of *Learning Their Language*, Marta works with clients by phone and email all over the world, providing intuitive consultations for all types of animals. She lives in Northern California and travels internationally to lecture, teach classes, and hold clinics on intuitive communication with animals and nature. To schedule a consultation or to find out about attending or hosting a class or clinic, please call her at 707-829-8186 or email her at marta@martawilliams.com. You can also visit her website at www.martawilliams.com.